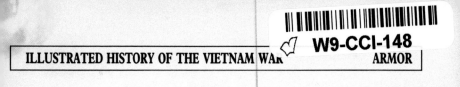

BANTAM BOOKS

TORONTO • NEW YORK • LONDON • SYDNEY • AUCKLAND

ARMOR
by
James R. Arnold

RENDEZVOUS
A pair of M-113 ACAVs head
cross-country for convoy escort duty

RECON BY FIRE

An M-113 ACAV squadron about to shatter the dawn with a 'mad minute' of fire to flush out the enemy.

WORKHORSE
IN
ARMOR

The M-113 armored personnel carrier was the utility vehicle of the war. Over 40,000 saw service in Vietnam.

EDITORS: Richard Ballantine, Richard Grant. PHOTO RESEARCH: John Moore.
DRAWINGS: John Batchelor. MAPS: Peter Williams. STUDIO: Kim Williams.
PRODUCED BY: The Up & Coming Publishing Company, Bearsville, New York.

ARMOR
THE ILLUSTRATED HISTORY OF THE VIETNAM WAR
A Bantam Book/ August 1987

ACKNOWLEDGEMENTS

*The author wishes to thank the many armor veterans who gave their time to
tell their stories: Ted Ballard, Walter Bradford, Bill Cooley, David Doyle,
Dudley Farquhar, Pete Harrington, Dick Lawrence, Jim Leach, James
Logan, and Duke Wolf.*

*Photographs for this book were selected from the archives of DAVA,
Military Archive Research Services, the USAF, and Sgt. Roger Welt.*

All rights reserved
Copyright © 1987 Rufus Publications, Inc.
*This book may not be reproduced in whole or in part, by mimeograph or
any other means, without permission.*
For information address: Bantam Books, Inc.

Library of Congress Cataloging-in-Publication Data

Arnold, James, 1923-
Armor.

(The Illustrated history of the Vietnam War)
1. Vietnamese Conflict, 1961-1975—Tank warfare.
I. Title. II. Series.
DS558.9.A75A76   1987   959.704′342   87-11526
ISBN 0-553-34347-5

Published simultaneously in the United States and Canada

*Bantam Books are published by Bantam Books, Inc. Its trademark, consisting of the
words "Bantam Books" and the portrayal of a rooster, is Registered in U.S. Patent
and Trademark Office and in other countries. Marca Registrada. Bantam Books, Inc.,
666 Fifth Avenue, New York, New York 10103.*

PRINTED IN THE UNITED STATES OF AMERICA

CW   0   9   8   7   6   5   4   3   2

Contents

No Place for Tanks?

Incident at Suoi Cat

IT ALWAYS comes down to the man on the spot, a front-line combat soldier trying to do his duty. On December 2, 1966, the man was Lieutenant Wilbert Radosevich; the spot, Suoi Cat, 30 miles east of Saigon. As Radosevich led his resupply convoy on the return trip from Blackhorse base camp, he definitely was not thinking about the extensive, often bitter debate that preceded the commitment of his unit, the 11th Armored Cavalry, to Vietnam. Instead the lieutenant focused on a more immediate problem. The small hamlet of Suoi Cat should have been full of people. When he had passed this way earlier, the village had pulsed with life. Now it was quiet. In particular there were no children playing along the road. Their absence worried Radosevich.

The convoy included the lieutenant's tank, followed by two modified M-113 personnel carriers, two trucks, another M-113, and a rear guard tank. The fact that any armored vehicles were in the convoy was a matter of great importance to a number of high-ranking officers both in Vietnam and back in the States. Only after armor had demonstrated its combat effectiveness had substantial numbers of tanks and other mechanized equipment been sent to Vietnam.

In the beginning, the Pentagon had decided that Vietnam would be an infantryman's war. They had believed that Vietnam was totally unsuited for armored combat. They cited the disasters inflicted upon French armor in an earlier war on the same terrain. The combination of mountains, jungle, and waterlogged paddy fields confined heavy vehicles to the road, the experts claimed. Roadbound mechanized units made highly vulnerable targets for ambush. Furthermore, what could conventional armored units accomplish against an enemy who used hit-and-

run raids, melting into the interior when opposed by superior strength?

This challenging question was exactly the proposition that some armored advocates wanted to answer. They recognized that since World War II, American armor doctrine had been preparing for a conventional war in Europe. As late as 1965, the Armor Officer Advanced Course never formally discussed Vietnam. At first it seemed this oversight would cause no problems. The high command in Vietnam was constrained by manpower limits set in Washington. As planners sorted through available options, the bias against employing armor remained high.

During 1965, as the American supreme commander, General William Westmoreland, began to recognize the difficulties he confronted, more American troops were requested. President Lyndon Johnson responded by raising manpower authorizations. For the first time armor was included on the menu of available units. Thus it was that Lieutenant Radosevich's 11th Armored Cavalry, the famous Blackhorse Regiment, entered Vietnam. Many skeptics wondered what it could accomplish. Years of military teaching, tactical debate, and armored equipment design had come down to this, a small armored convoy about to engage the vaunted Viet Cong.

The battle began, as many do, with an accident. After ensuring that he was in radio contact with an air controller flying overhead in a helicopter, Radosevich turned inside his tank's turret in order to look around. He bumped the turret control handle, sending the turret slowly revolving to one side. Just in front of his tank a tremendous explosion rocked the ground. A nervous enemy, startled by the tank turret's sudden motion, had prematurely detonated a mine. This signaled the Viet Cong unit to open fire from hidden positions along the road.

The lieutenant reacted quickly to alert the reserves back at base that the convoy had encountered the enemy. "Ambush! Ambush! Claymore Corner!" he shouted into his radio. Everyone in Radosevich's squadron knew where "Claymore Corner" was without consulting a map. If Radosevich's convoy could hold on, help would soon arrive.

Radosevich revved his tank's engine and ordered

Packed 10,000 to a "beehive" round these inch-long steel fléchettes cut through the air like a hail of porcupine quills. Deadly up to 300 yards beehive was

also used to strip down dense vegetation and detonate mines. This type of canister earned its nickname from the frightening buzzing noise the dart-like nails made as they scythed through the air.

the convoy to follow his lead. Driving at full speed through the fireswept area, they charged forward along the road. The tank cannons and machineguns blasted back at the unseen enemy. Viet Cong fire remained heavy. A personnel carrier, already hit three times, was hit once more and burst into flame just as the convoy neared the far edge of the fire zone.

Radosevich's radio alert stimulated an immediate, three-pronged American response. From the air, a helicopter swooped down to provide covering fire. Simultaneously, the air controller called for assistance. Back at camp, a tank company, a cavalry unit, and a self-propelled howitzer battery rushed out the gates in just eight minutes to head for the convoy. Another cavalry unit, Troop B, headed towards the ambush from the opposite direction.

Troop B reached the action just as the convoy cleared the fire zone. In the best cavalry tradition it immediately counterattacked, and instantly met a hail of fire. Troop B halted, with vehicles alternately facing opposite sides of the road, and fired back. When the Viet Cong fire grew too heavy, they moved on. By these fire-and-move tactics Troop B fought clear of the ambush while covering the convoy's escape.

Ten minutes into the fight, Radosevich's squadron commander arrived overhead in another helicopter. He took control of the battle, designating that one side of the road would receive air strikes while the other would be bombarded by the howitzers. Following this brief softening up, he ordered Troop B, now reinforced by tanks and armored personnel carriers from the base, to charge back into the ambush.

This time the cavalry proceeded more systematically. The 90mm tank guns fired canister against enemy infantry who had been forced from their positions by the bombardment. The bursting shotgun-like spread of the canister's steel darts mowed down the exposed enemy. The Viet Cong tried to set up a recoilless rifle to knock out the American tanks. Instead, a pointblank round of canister knocked the rifle out. Armored vehicles surrounded the ambush site, catching the enemy in a crossfire. As darkness came, the battered guerrillas abandoned the field.

The significance of the Suoi Cat action lay not in the enemy losses, although the Viet Cong suffered

Tank commander Lt. Wilbert Radosevich —his successful counterattack against a Viet Cong ambush at Suoi Cat led to a reappraisal of armored tactics. Subsequently Lt. Radosevich was awarded the Silver Star for gallantry.

fairly heavily. Rather the successful use of armor tactics was the important lesson. Armored vehicles could absorb the pounding that came from an ambush long enough to escort a convoy clear of the kill zone. Then, after re-grouping, they could re-enter fireswept ground in a mobile counterattack aimed at the flanks of the ambush. Combining fire and movement with the shock value of charging armored vehicles, armor could turn the tables on an immobile enemy who was dug in on fixed lines. In association with air and artillery support, this method proved an effective tactical response to enemy ambushes.

The unsuccessful ambush of Lieutenant Radosevich's convoy in 1966 demonstrated that fighting armored vehicles could provide valuable service in Vietnam. It would take another three years to silence most of the skeptics. By then armor was playing an increasingly important role in American military plans.

The first American troops to enter Vietnam were ordered to leave their tanks behind. The turnaround in tactical thinking is well illustrated by the fact that the last major unit sent to Vietnam was an armored unit, the 1st Brigade, 5th Infantry Division (Mechanized). When American units began to be withdrawn and sent back home, armor remained. The high command had learned that in numerous situations, tanks and other armored vehicles were without equal. By the end, tankers, cavalrymen, and mechanized infantry had proven their worth.

SERVING NOTICE: Early propaganda leaflet issued by the Blackhorse and drawn by a Vietnamese artist.

VIỆT-CỘNG
HÃY COI CHỪNG!!

"Viet Cong Beware! No place to run! No place to hide! It is too late now! The tanks of the mighty 11th Armored Cavalry Regiment will seek you out and destroy you. Your only chance to live is to rally to the RVN Government. Rally to live or hide and die."

Into the Fire Zone

WHEN THE French command made the fateful decision in late 1953 to commit a major force to an obscure valley airstrip named Dien Bien Phu, the obstacles to using armor seemed overwhelming. Nevertheless, to give the base some offensive punch ten American built Chaffee tanks were airlifted in. Since the tanks' weight exceeded the capacity of any single plane, the vehicles were disassembled into 180 separate bundles, the bundles flown to Dien Bien Phu, and reassembled in a field near the airstrip.

Very little could be done to redress the several incredible blunders that prompted the French to place a major base in the bottom of a distant, fog-enshrouded valley where the enemy held the high ground. Yet the ten tanks almost proved a tactical trump card. After the event, observers would ponder whether a few more tanks might have turned the tide.

From fixed positions, the tanks helped anchor the defense. Leading counterattacks against the entrenched enemy, they demonstrated their worth. During one counterattack, one tank was hit six times by recoilless rifle fire but kept running. Five days later a bazooka round penetrated the hull, wounding two men. The men were replaced and the tank kept going. Ten days passed and it received a bazooka round in the turret, killing two men. In spite of being shelled, bazookaed, and mined, this vehicle and five others remained in action to the end.

Less than 5 percent of the French forces in Indochina were lost at Dien Bien Phu. However, the psychological impact was similar to that of the Tet Offensive 14 years later. The French tried to continue the war much like the Americans after Tet,

17

Into the fire zone

M24 CHAFFEE LIGHT TANK:

Light and maneuverable World War II vet. Phased out in 1964 as breakdowns became more frequent and spare parts less available.

in hopes of favorably influencing peace talks. Since 1951, the French had increasingly relied upon task forces called Groupement Mobiles, or Mobile Groups, as their active field units. These were road-bound regimental size units that contained only small numbers of tanks and other armored vehicles. When Mobile Group 100 was destroyed in a series of deadly jungle ambushes following the fall of Dien Bien Phu, it seemed to indicate that armor was ill-suited for this type of war. Yet Mobile Group 100 contained only one squadron of obsolete, World War II era tanks. The bulk of the regiment travelled in unarmored, open trucks.

In any military examination of French involvement in Indochina, critics falsely equated the French

COMBAT TAXI:

The M-113 armored personnel carrier (APC) quickly became the basic compact of the war. Fast, light and versatile it gave rise to some sixty variants. Intended as a ''combat taxi'' to deliver troops into the fire zone, the 12-man vehicle quickly proved itself in action to be an agile assault vehicle in its own right. With a watertight hull, rubber seals on all doors, and two bilge pumps to keep the inside dry, the M-113 could switch from road to water without preparation. Rubber blades on its tracks propelled it through water at 3.5 mph.

term 'groupement mobile' with armored force and thereby drew incorrect conclusions.

The destruction of roadbound French mechanized units, notably Mobile Group 100, overshadowed the real contributions armor had made. Certain well planned armored sweeps had been successful, and the tanks at Dien Bien Phu had been invaluable bulwarks for the base's defense.

The disasters stood out. The successes were largely forgotten. Indochina became known as a place armor should avoid, a place where armor could contribute little, a place where armor ran grave risks when caught in fearsome, destructive ambushes. Yet these lessons from a losing side greatly influenced how the American Army fought its war in Vietnam.

Despite the peacetime overtones of this 1962 US Army publicity photo, most armor advisers attached to Military Assistance Command Vietnam (MACV) saw action. Rules of engagement forbade them to fire until fired upon. In the early years US advisers re-organised ARVN armored units along US lines into cavalry regiments consisting of one tank and two reconnaissance squadrons.

WHEN the first American military advisers arrived in 1956, they found the South Vietnamese armored forces to be a rag-tag lot. Their vehicles were French hand-me-downs, their tactics stressed static defense. Although the Americans began an extensive reorganization, not until 1962 did Vietnamese armored units become a force to be reckoned with.

Part of this improvement was due to training and part to the arrival of new equipment. Included in the latter were the relatively new M-113 armored personnel carriers, or APCs. These impressive vehicles had been designed with a conventional war in Europe in mind. They were intended to solve a historic problem confronted by the infantry since the development of accurate massed shell and bullet fire: how to ensure that soldiers could cross a fireswept zone and close with the enemy.

In World War II, experience showed that tanks could advance through all but the heaviest shell fire while their armor plating made them immune to machine guns and other small arms. The hapless infantry who tried to go with them would all too often be killed or pinned down. Consequently, the tanks and infantry became separated as the tanks continued to advance. Then the tanks would fall prey in turn to the enemy infantry, who could approach to close range with rocket launchers and similar weapons.

To solve this problem the M-113 had been developed. Its armored walls allowed infantry to ride across a fire zone in relative safety. Then they would dismount and assault the enemy. But this tactical doctrine was developed for hypothetical, large-scale armored combats in Europe. How well the APC would work in Vietnam was a major question.

Early results were disappointing. The first vehicles were placed in the hands of poorly trained troops who failed to exploit the APC's capabilities. But slowly they gained experience, and with it came significant battlefield successes.

When the Army of the Republic of Vietnam (ARVN) 7th Infantry Division planned a major operation in the Plain of Reeds, one American adviser had serious doubts about its practicality. Captain Bricker noted that the division's mechanized company would have to operate in waterlogged rice paddies. He doubted they could. Since the plan had been developed personally by the Vietnamese division commander, Bricker's objections were overridden.

Shortly before 11 a.m. on September 25, 1962, nine APCs found themselves looking for a place to ford a small canal. Suddenly, a nearby unit spotted a group of Viet Cong (VC). The ARVN company commander, Captain Ly Tong Ba, ordered an attack. Bricker advised that the company maneuver against the enemy's flanks. Instead, the intrepid Captain Ba ordered a frontal charge right through the flooded paddies.

As the APCs splashed ahead, throwing up sheets of mud and water, surprised Viet Cong soldiers began popping up from concealed positions. Some fired their weapons, others ran in fear. The South Vietnamese soldiers fired at them from open hatches. The .50-caliber machine gun mounted atop the M-113 swept the field. Manning these guns took courage. The slightly built ARVN machine gunners had to sit exposed on top of the APC since they could only cock the heavy weapon by bracing themselves against the hatch cover. In so doing they were completely exposed to return fire.

Then as they were chasing the scattered enemy the American adviser intervened.

Following conventional American doctrine he insisted that the South Vietnamese should dismount and fight from the ground as they had now closed

LONG CONTROLS, SHORT TRUST: The downside of the decision to use aluminum to make the M-113 air transportable was the increased risk of mine damage. Disregarding orders to ride inside, drivers devised these ''long controls'' to allow them to steer from on top. The price was a high casualty rate from enemy gunfire. Later versions were fitted with titanium base shields to encourage crews to stay inside.

U S ARMY
13D-061

ABOVE:
After the overthrow of President Ngo Dinh Diem armor was stationed at palace gates and street corners.

with the enemy. After a lengthy debate Bricker persuaded his ARVN counterpart to order his men off the vehicles. It was a mistake.

While the ARVN forces were moving and shooting, the VC could not fire effectively at them. When they dismounted, the ARVN forces lost this advantage. As they wallowed in knee-deep mud, the enemy rallied. The guerrillas moved to concealed high spots in the paddy, where their firepower began to inflict serious losses on the immobilized ARVN.

After a painful hour the action ended and the mechanized troops remounted. As they moved off they again attracted hostile fire. The APCs charged again but this time the men stayed inside their vehicles. The VC were flushed from concealed posi-

VOTING MACHINES: Tanks and APCs were frequent visitors in the streets of Saigon during the political upheavals that led to four changes of the South Vietnamese government in five years. Accused of political intimidation by their enemies, many ARVN mechanized units were nicknamed "coup troops" and their tanks dubbed "voting machines". Ironically ARVN armored forces gained their first experience of tank vs. tank warfare during the successful coup against President Ngo Dinh Diem when tanks of the palace guard engaged the ARVN 4th Cavalry Regiment in battle.

tions and overrun by the fast-moving APCs. As the action ended, over 100 enemy dead were found, together with a considerable haul of abandoned weapons, indicating they had fled in panic.

The M-113s hadn't been employed as their designers intended, yet things had worked out remarkably well. Here was a lesson. Armored fighting vehicles could successfully maneuver on difficult ground and combine firepower with shock action to rout a veteran foe.

In the years that followed, doctrine was changed to emphasize mounted rather than dismounted combat. The M-113 became an assault vehicle instead of merely a "combat taxi" and gained a reputation as an outstanding armored vehicle.

Red Beach

IT WAS clear by the first months of 1965, despite the presence of some 20,000 American 'advisors' and the high quality of some of its units, that the ARVN was fighting a losing battle. The US government felt it had no alternative to sending in combat troops if the tide of communism was to be held back.

So it was that US Marines once again led their country's forces into battle. With TV cameras rolling, the landing craft approached their target, yet another Red Beach 2 on yet another foreign shore. The historical significance of this landing, the first in a new war onto a color-coded beach whose very name stirred memories of the assaults through fire-swept surf during World War II, may not have occurred to Marine Corps Staff Sergeant John Downey. However, he probably shared some of the nervous tension experienced by other Marines who had made assault landings. The landing craft shuddered to a halt in the shallows. Its front ramp dropped and Downey gunned the engine on his big Patton tank. The first American armored unit had entered Vietnam.

When Battalion Landing Team 3/9 splashed ashore on Red Beach 2 just north of Da Nang on March 8, 1965, they were received by groups of pretty, giggling Vietnamese girls laden with welcoming wreaths of red and yellow flowers. On the beach stood a sign with the sarcastic message announcing that Red Beach 2 had been "secured" by a combat engineer group. In spite of the peaceful landing, American soldiers had in fact entered a shooting war. Besides the tanks, other armored vehicles participated in this first landing. Indeed, the initial wave of assault troops came ashore in 11 LVT-5 "amtrac" armored amphibians, giant 35-ton vehicles capable of swimming through water and then running on tracks once ashore. Offshore, additional tanks and Ontos (meaning "the thing" in Greek),

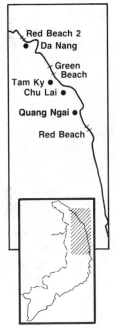

Red Beach

TURNING POINT:
March 8, 1965.
The first US
combat troops
land. But for
the 3,500
Marines,
Da Nang's Red
Beach 2 was
an anticlimax.
General
Westmoreland
commented
that they were
dressed "as if
re-enacting Iwo
Jima." Yet the
only obstacle
encountered
was a
welcoming
party of
giggling
Vietnamese
college girls
bearing
garlands of
flowers.

tracked antitank vehicles, remained in reserve. Wave conditions prevented the immediate commitment of all these units, but when they did come ashore they moved right into a controversy.

The American ambassador, Maxwell Taylor of World War II fame, the Pentagon, and President Johnson were in accordance that American forces were needed to help secure the growing American bases in Vietnam. When troops were requested, no one in authority carefully examined the composition of the Marine landing team. Thus, both Taylor and the Pentagon were surprised to see TV film showing American tanks driving onto the shores of Vietnam.

Taylor vehemently protested, saying the tanks were "not appropriate for counterinsurgency operations". The Marines did not agree. They felt there

was no reason to change their standard operational procedure. So, by default rather than by planning, American armor entered the war; an inauspicious beginning that foreshadowed the reluctance of many American commanders to recognize armor's value.

After occupying their defensive perimeters, the Marines spent their first weeks ashore learning to adjust to a very tough environment. Heat and humidity proved a greater enemy than anything else. Consequently, at first patrolling and heavy work were restricted to the cooler hours of early morning and late afternoon. Slowly the Marines acclimatized as the commanders sorted through intelligence estimates and prepared plans. Then it became time to strike.

It appeared that the 1st VC Regiment intended to attack the important base at Chu Lai. A deserter

27

THE THING:
The Onto
*(Greek for
"the thing")*
was designed
as a light, air-
portable
antitank
weapon. With
no enemy
tanks to
confront, Ontos
proved most
effective in the
streetfighting
in Hue, where
they could dart
down alleys
too narrow for
tanks, fire their
six 106mm
recoilless
rifles, retreat,
and reload.

revealed the location of his regiment's headquarters to be in a coastal village complex 12 miles south of Chu Lai. Faced with the choice of waiting for the enemy to strike or hitting him first, the Marines reacted with characteristic aggressiveness. A multi-pronged attack was planned featuring Marines attacking from the sea while others landed behind the village complex from helicopters to trap the VC between two fires. Operation Starlite, the largest American ground action to date, and the first regimental size U.S. operation since the Korean War, was born.

Starlite called for the 3d Battalion, 3d Marines to land on Green Beach and advance inland to meet up with the forces landing by helicopter. Five M-48 tanks and three M-67 flame tanks—basic M-48 tanks equipped with flame guns instead of 90mm guns, capable of effectively shooting a jet of fire some 150 yards—provided armored support for the amphibious assault.

Following a short naval bombardment, Companies I and K rode their LVTs across Green Beach and headed inland. The LVTs, with their 11-foot-high silhouettes glistening with salt water, presented a formidable sight as they trundled across the beach,

dropped their ramps, and disgorged green-clad Marines. A charge exploded in front of one LVT that was pressing inland, but it caused no damage. The first objective, An Cuong 1, proved empty of enemy soldiers. More tanks and Ontos vehicles, bizarre-looking but nimble 9-ton tracked vehicles carrying six recoilless rifles, came ashore to help secure a defensive perimeter. Meanwhile, as the air mobile and seaborne columns converged, VC resistance increased.

Company H commander Lieutenant Homer Jenkins led his men toward An Cuong 2 across open rice paddies. Accompanying his men were five tanks and three Ontos. Mistakenly believing a nearby village had been cleared, Jenkins entered an area between two small hills. Rifle and machine gun fire caught Company H in a vicious cross fire. Exploding mortar rounds pelted the Americans. Adding to the problems, the tracked vehicles started sliding around in the waterlogged paddies and seemed about to become bogged down.

Jenkins wisely ordered his armor to form a tight circle, behind which he sheltered his infantry. Outside this perimeter, a detached squad waged a gallant fight against a VC mortar position. After knocking it out and killing nine enemy soldiers, the unit became pinned down by heavy shell and automatic weapons fire. Suddenly a barrage of white phosphorous grenades hit.

It appeared the Marines would be overrun when Lance Corporal Joe C. Paul stood up and placed himself between his wounded comrades and the enemy fire. He opened fire to such effect that the VC barrage was momentarily suppressed. Although critically hit himself, Paul continued firing in order to cover the evacuation of the other wounded to the cover of the armored vehicles. Then he collapsed. Lance Corporal Paul posthumously received the Congressional Medal of Honor since "By his fortitude and gallant spirit of self-sacrifice in the face of almost certain death, he saved the lives of several of his fellow Marines."

Lieutenant Jenkins successfully withdrew his force under cover of an air strike. Meanwhile, headquarters organized a supply column to succor another battered company. This resupply force comprised five LVTs and three flame tanks. Although

US Ambassador Maxwell Taylor —questioned the deployment of American ground troops. A former chairman of the Joint Chiefs of Staff, he warned that "white-faced" soldiers were not suitable for "Asian forests and jungles."

Red Beach

The M-48A3 Patton was the first diesel powered version of the tank first introduced in the Korean War. With its boat-shaped hull it could ford waters up to seven feet deep with the aid of a snorkel.

a staff officer thought he had thoroughly briefed this group on how to get to the objective, once it set off it quickly got lost. The column was following a trail flanked on one side by hedge rows and the other by a rice paddy. The two leading vehicles had just passed a bend in the trail when suddenly an explosion rocked the middle of the column. Simultaneously, rocket and mortar rounds tore into the Marines. Then the VC infantry charged.

The tanks and LVTs maneuvered to use their weapons. When the gunner on the rear flame tank tried to fire, he found an enemy shell had wrecked the barrel. Meanwhile, the Marine command post received word over the radio network that the convoy was being overrun. They were, however, unable

THE UNWANTED: The arrival of these Marine Corps M48 tanks came as a rude surprise to US ambassador Taylor. Tanks were inappropriate for counter-insurgency operations, he complained.

to determine the exact details, because a panic-stricken LVT radio operator kept his microphone button depressed the entire time while pleading for help. This action prevented any communication on that radio frequency. Various elements inherent in the friction of war were conspiring to make the muddled situation increasingly perilous.

Faced with Jenkins' beleagered unit isolated and in trouble, and now the resupply convoy apparently being overrun, the operational commander, Colonel Oscar Peatross, assisted by Andrew Comer, hastily arranged another relief column. An improvised rescue force would be based on "a rapidly moving tank, LVT, and Ontos column." At 1 pm this second relief force set out. Breasting a small hill, the

Red Beach

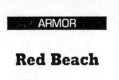

AMTRAC CROSSING: With most of its 11-foot hull submerged, a Marine amtrac (amphibian tractor) transports troops across the Ca De Son River in I Corps, the military region closest to North Vietnam. The amtracs had been intended for beach assaults, but with US landings unopposed, the amtracs were redeployed as armored personnel carriers as the Marines began to sweep inland from their coastal bases. Like the infantry's M-113, the amtrac had a watertight hull and could float on its tracks.

lead tank received a hit from a recoilless rifle and shuddered to a halt. The following vehicles jammed together and became targets for intense mortar bombardment coupled with saturating small arms fire. Within minutes five Marines died and 17 suffered wounds.

Undaunted, the surviving infantry dismounted while the Ontos maneuvered to provide supporting fire from their multiple-barrel recoilless rifles. The enemy fire slackened, but by now the nature of the VC tactics had become apparent. As Comer stated, "It was obvious that the VC were deeply dug in, and emerged above ground when we presented them with an opportunity and withdrew whenever we retaliated or threatened them."

Eventually, additional Marine reinforcements forced the VC to break contact. Of the 23 men in the resupply convoy, only nine remained in action throughout the three-hour engagement. Some 60 dead VC lay on the ground around their vehicles.

At this early stage in the war, body counts were conscientiously performed. In Operation Starlite the Marines had killed over 600 VC at a cost of 45 dead

Col. Oscar F. Peatross —commander of the Regimental Landing Team (RLT-7) during Operation Starlite. RLT-7 was later awarded the Navy Unit Commendation for "outstanding heroism against enemy Viet Cong forces."

and 203 wounded. While the action had been characterized by confusion common to soldiers entering their first combat, this new generation of Marines had shown the same bravery that had made the Corps an elite fighting force.

Armor had been crucial in keeping American losses down. Colonel Peatross commented that "the tanks were certainly the difference between extremely heavy casualties and the number that we actually took." And the tanks had been in the center of the action: "Every place the tanks went, they drew a crowd of VC." Although many vehicles were temporarily knocked out, all were repaired after the battle.

Just as the Americans had made some understandable rookie mistakes, so the VC assessed their battlefield performance. Soon, they would avoid combat with American armor whenever possible.

While all concerned were digesting the lessons of combat, the American buildup continued. By the end of 1965, 65 M-48 tanks, 12 flame tanks, 65 Ontos, and 157 amphibian tractors had arrived in the Marine Corps area.

Ambush! Ambush!

New tactics and techniques

THE MARINES took their tanks into battle with them as a matter of course. When US Army units entered into Vietnam in 1965 the American commander, General William C. Westmoreland, confronted a strict ceiling on troop numbers. He placed armor low on his list of priorities. It took six months and some hard fighting to change his mind.

The first major debate about armor arose when the 1st Infantry Division—The Big Red One of World War II fame—prepared for commitment. Organized for a nuclear battlefield in Europe, the division included two tank battalions, mechanized units (infantry who rode into battle aboard armored personnel carriers), and a divisional armored cavalry squadron. Planners decided that almost all armor would be left behind.

The Army chief of staff allowed only the divisional cavalry, the 1st Squadron, 4th Cavalry (1/4 Cav) to keep their medium M-48 tanks to test the effectiveness of armor. General Westmoreland believed the test would fail: "Vietnam is no place for either tank or mechanized infantry units."

Those who shared Westmoreland's opinion pointed out that a mechanized battalion required 900 soldiers while a dismounted infantry battalion required 100 fewer. Furthermore, the mech infantry needed another 150 men for maintenance as well as additional men to guard the repair shops and garages. Similarly, a tank battalion required 570 men, of whom only 220 were actual combatants. The majority supported the minority who actually fought. Given the severe constraints posed by manpower ceilings, it seemed clear that armor offered "less bang for the buck."

Amid this climate of extreme skepticism, the

35

Track driver William Burnett —single-handedly— unjammed a machine gun to stop a VC advance. His bravery won him the Silver Star.

first Army armored unit, the 1/4 Cav, arrived in Vietnam.

This proud unit's first six months in Vietnam were extremely frustrating. Its components were scattered all over the map while the tanks were held back at base. Consequently, it was unable to fight as a unit. Finally, on the evening of November 11, 1965, armor got a chance to show its worth.

A mechanized task force moved into a nighttime defensive perimeter near Ap Bau Bang. During the day the unit had experienced no enemy contact. Rolls of barbed wire were laid out around the perimeter while the infantry dug individual foxholes. A reasonable field of fire was created all around the perimeter and listening posts were set out. Minutes after dawn, 50 to 60 mortar rounds slammed into the perimeter, wounding two men. Nothing happened for another 30 minutes. Suddenly, violent enemy fire swept over the defenders. Under cover of this fire, the Viet Cong moved to within 40 yards of the waiting Americans. They seemed confident they were about to maul the inexperienced cavalrymen.

The roar of gasoline engines added to the racket. APCs of the 3d Platoon charged out from the perimeter and smashed into the startled enemy assault troops. The violent counterattack totally disrupted the VC attack. Nonetheless, the veteran enemy infantry regrouped and mounted a second assault from some rubber trees against the opposite side of the perimeter. Supported by mortar and machine gun fire, they crawled through waist-high bushes toward the defenders.

A gap appeared in the defensive line when a .500-caliber machine gun on top of an APC jammed The VC surged forward. Specialist 4 William Burnett, a track driver (soldiers called the armored personnel carriers "tracks") left the shelter of his driving compartment to clamber atop his vehicle. He cleared the jammed weapon and opened fire at point-blank range. Fourteen enemy soldiers fell before his gun. Burnett's fire broke the back of this enemy attack.

The gallant Viet Cong did not give up. Into the teeth of American air strikes, they resumed the attack. Several times the American tracks moved to plug a hole in the line. One VC squad breached the wire and overran an artillery position. A counterattack drove them out.

Finally, after a six-hour fight the enemy withdrew. Seven cavalrymen had been killed and 35 wounded. Two M-113s and three M-106 mortar carriers had been wrecked and another three damaged. But the ability of the tracks to maneuver under fire—when they made their initial sortie out from the perimeter and later when they moved around to block enemy penetrations—had been impressive. The 1st Squadron, 4th Cavalry, had made the case for armored forces.

The high command realized that armor had a useful role to play in Vietnam. General Westmoreland would write: "The ability of mechanized cavalry to operate effectively in the Vietnamese countryside convinced me that I was mistaken in a belief that modern armor had only a limited role in the fighting in Vietnam." Consequently, additional American armor units soon entered the war.

THROUGH mid-1966, American armor remained largely roadbound. From a technical standpoint, the cross-country ability of armored fighting vehicles depended on power, traction, and flotation. Both the M-48 (Patton) tank and the M-113 had engine and

THE MAKING OF THE ACAV: Combat experience quickly demonstrated the need for more protection for M-113 crews. In 1966 a kit comprised of this "bathtub" all-around protective shield for the commander's .50 Browning plus two side-mounted M60 machine guns upgraded the M-113 into the ACAV (Armored Cavalry Assault Vehicle).

Ambush!
Ambush!

JUNGLE BUSTERS:
Tanks proved effective in penetrating dense jungle for search-and-destroy operations, although this M483A lost part of its fender in the process. Infantry rode on the tanks to increase mobility and decrease exposure to mines. But officers worried that one well-placed rocket could annihilate a tightly packed group.

transmission systems that delivered ample power to the tracks.

Traction was a different problem. The caterpillar track used by American armor differed very little from the type of tracks used on the first tanks in World War I. Essentially, the track was a design compromise between traction in mud and efficiency on the sprawling road networks of Europe. Consequently, they could all too easily bog down in rice paddy, stream, or swamp.

Mud mobility was a function of traction and flotation. A vehicle with a low ground pressure would keep its hull and suspension system above the ground's surface. The M-113 had a low ground pressure and was thus able to operate even in pad-

dies of standing water. A Patton tank, with ground pressure half again as great, would mire in the same terrain.

Exaggerated fears over bogging down unduly limited armored deployment until cavalrymen and tankers gained more experience. Consequently, in the early years they mostly operated on roads and trails. It was there that the Viet Cong /North Vietnamese Army (VC/NVA) tried to destroy them. The road ambush became the first great tactical challenge for American armor.

Beginning in the summer of 1966, the 1st Infantry Division began a series of operations to open Route 13 from Saigon to Binh Long Province near the Cambodian border. One of these triggered the

Sgt. Donald Long—during the Battle of Srok Dong he braved enemy gunfire to rescue the wounded. When a grenade landed among them the 29-year-old cavalryman threw himself on it to absorb the blast. He was posthumously awarded the Medal of Honor for saving "the lives of eight comrades at the expense of his own life."

Battle of Srok Dong, which was destined to be one of the classic engagements of the Vietnam War.

Troop B of the 1/4 Cav moved along Route 13 in the stifling heat of June 30. The cavalry was one of the few tank-equipped units serving in Vietnam at this time. Without warning, heavy enemy fire struck the column. The troop's four tanks received hits from concealed recoilless rifles that clanged against turret-top cupolas decapitating the exposed tank commanders, and killing or wounding their crews. APCs rushed forward to help, their decks laden with infantrymen. A rain of mortar shells blew them off the vehicles. In the resulting confusion, a traffic jam frustrated all efforts to maneuver.

Troop C tried to move around this jam, only to have its lead tank sustain a direct hit. Two heavily wounded men were removed and the column regrouped and managed to continue. Thick brush overlapping the road prevented the Americans from seeing the VC who fought from jungle cover. Troopers aimlessly lobbed grenades out of their vehicles in an effort to neutralize the heavy enemy fire.

The same lead tank was hit again. This time a wounded gunner was removed, leaving only a sergeant to carry on. He continued to spearhead Troop C's advance until finally they came up to Troop B at the ambush site. Three new crewmen joined the lone sergeant in the lead tank. Together, they fought through the burning wrecks of the battered cavalrymen to arrive at a central position that commanded the area. Since power to the tank's turret had been knocked out, the perspiring crew manually rotated the heavy turret so it could fire effectively. In this manner, the makeshift crew fired all 60 rounds of the tank's basic load. Troop C's tracks, inspired by this example, formed up around Troop B to shield them from further damage.

At last Troop B withdrew to a crossroad where helicopters arrived to evacuate dead and wounded. Even here they were not safe. A sniper round struck a lieutenant who stood partially exposed in his hatch. Enemy pressure intensified and several more troopers were shot. As a mechanized flame thrower intervened, infantry reinforcements arrived by helicopter. The first chopper struck an unexploded American bomb and burst into flame. Undaunted, subsequent helicopters landed to deploy the reinforcements. As they did so, the VC broke contact.

Under extreme pressure, the 1/4 Cav had survived. The unit had maintained its gallant tradition. Many tactics could be successfully improvised in the field. But ideally, good training eliminates much of the need for such improvisation. More than one armor leader found "no relationship between straight armor doctrine as taught in the States and in Germany and the Vietnam experience." No armor school taught armor officers how to run convoys. No field manual addressed search-and-destroy missions. Consequently, officers often had to learn by doing. Against a veteran foe, it could be a costly education.

THE WAR was being called an "area war," meaning there were no clearly marked front lines and no completely safe rear areas. So it wasn't just the cavalry who had to learn how to handle ambushes; even soldiers assigned as drivers for convoy duty sometimes experienced combat. As soldiers were finding out throughout Vietnam, armor could be very helpful when the shooting began. The men in the 8th Transportation Group didn't have any armor assigned to them, so they made their own.

The work week is seven days long. The 8th Group soldier rises each morning for maintenance, guard duty, or to drive convoy. Today he will drive. It is another brilliant blue-sky day. A few puffy white clouds dot the sky. It will be hot. But probably sometime during the day he will be rained on. If it's the dry season in the lowlands, the rains will fall as he climbs into the highlands. If the monsoon rains are over in the highlands, he will catch it on the flatland. Heat, rain, monotony—three constants in his life.

Following breakfast the driver goes to the motor pool where he receives his green log book and manifest. The log lists his truck's mileage and maintenance schedule, the manifest identifies the cargo. After finding out what he is carrying his first thought is "Can I use it?" A cargo of 105mm artillery rounds has little value to the common soldier. C-rations, cigarettes, or toiletries are useful items that help make the tour more tolerable.

Climbing into his cab, the driver dons his flak jacket and steel pot helmet. He will keep them on until passing the checkpoint at the base's exit.

Armored flatbed—The need for a fast armored all-terrain cargo carrier led to the introduction of the M-548 transporter. Developed from the M-113A1's power pack suspension, and tracks, the M-548 had a six-ton payload and a top speed of 42 mph. The M66 machine gun and rear hoist were fitted as standard.

Ambush! Ambush!

HERRINGBONE FORMATION: During the battle of the Minh Thanh road—one of the first major ambushes of the war—tanks took up firing positions with vehicles alternately facing left and right. This allowed them to protect both flanks and fire against an enemy positioned on both sides of the road. The tactic proved successful, and "herringboning" quickly became the standard response of all armored units when ambushed.

There's a $25 fine if caught not wearing them. But as soon as he can he will take the helmet off. The 2.5-ton truck's motion over bumpy roads causes helmet to bounce off his brow ridge and nose. Besides the cuts and bruises, the helmet is hot to wear. His rifle is secured on a stand next to the gearshift.

The trucks form up at Camp Addison's trailer transfer point where each vehicle is assigned its position in the convoy. Facing east means Bong Son. Today the convoy faces west, they are heading for Pleiku. It will take half a day to travel the 100 miles there.

The stacatto bursts of heavy weapons interrupts the early morning calm. The driver ignores the sound. It's the gun trucks firing off a few rounds to check their guns. The armored trucks take station. Six of them, with names like Eve of Destruction,

Bounty Hunter, and VC Undertaker, protect the unarmored transport vehicles. They are a recent addition to the convoy, a response to a destructive ambush that occurred a month ago.

The 75-truck convoy lurches to a start. Driving west along Route 19 they leave the security of the camp. On the open road the driver swerves slightly to avoid a small pile of garbage on the road. He's been told the enemy likes to place mines under trash, boards, or cans in the road. The enemy knows that young GIs like to crush whatever they find in the road. It breaks the monotony. Prudent drivers don't do it.

The convoy gathers momentum, reaching nearly 45 miles per hour. Suddenly the pace dramatically slows. It's bumper-to-bumper in the dust. For no apparent reason speed picks up again. This is convoy

Ambush!
Ambush!

REFUELING RENDEZVOUS: Early VC hits on gasoline-powered ACAVs turned them into firebombs. The high command response was to convert all M-113s in Vietnam from gasoline to diesel power in the space of 11 months. Apart from reducing the fire risk the new diesel-powered M-113A1s had a greater range. With 95-gallon tanks they could cover up to 300 miles between refuelling stops.

rhythm played accordionlike, in fits and halts. At the An Khe rest stop the drivers stretch their legs, buy drinks from the Vietnamese soda girls, smoke, and talk. Someone reports he received a couple of rounds from a sniper. No one is surprised, it happens every day.

They climb back in. Now the road is beginning to climb into the highlands. Once they enter An Khe Pass, seven miles away, the road will be full of hairpin curves. They call it ambush alley.

The convoy slows again. A jeep goes by, the driver yelling "Sniper fire." The driver nods and waits. Over the idle of the engine he hears explosions. Probably friendly artillery rounds hitting somewhere nearby, fired by the protective fire bases that line the route. His truck creeps forward, approaching a small rise. From beyond the crest he sees black smoke rising.

He sees first a few, then several drivers abandoning their vehicles and diving into the roadside ditch. The line of opening truck doors and sprawling drivers looks like a line of dominoes toppling one another as he approaches. Grabbing his rifle, he too gets out of his truck.

Lying in the ditch he hears small-arms fire. The drivers are firing across the adjacent field. The field is mostly cleared, the result of American efforts to limit cover for potential ambushes. But the job hasn't been done perfectly. Mounds of dead underbrush dot the field. From behind one of these come some soldiers.

Some of the approaching soldiers wear red scarves while others wear helmets. The driver thinks it's all a mistake. These must be ARVN and our own men are shooting at them, he thinks. The firing gets more

INSET:
To overcome the shortage of gas tankers, diesel fuel was air-dropped in rubber blivitts at prearranged rendezvous points.

Specialist 4 Larry Dahl— served aboard a gun truck sent to rescue an ambushed convoy. When a grenade landed on his vehicle, machine gunner Dahl threw himself on it to absorb the blast. For this act of "conspicuous gallantry" he was awarded a posthumous Congressional Medal of Honor.

intense. He can see them clearer now. He can see them talking, hear their voices. They are approaching at a walk. They are the enemy, yet it's not like he had imagined. It's not like the combat scenes on the TV of his boyhood, nor like "Gallant Men" or "Combat." He opens fire . . . and suddenly they are gone. It's as if the ground itself has opened up and swallowed them.

OUT OF sight, on the far side of the rise where the black smoke rises, the gun trucks have fought their first battle.

It began when the lead truck spotted a linked chain of mines blocking the road. Recognizing they were entering an ambush, Jerry Christopher shouted to his driver, "We're in the kill zone!" It took a second for the driver to react. Only when he heard again, "We're in an ambush," did he gun the engine. The machine gunner standing in the back yelled, "let's give 'em hell!" but it was a little late.

A rocket smashed into the gun truck's front end, blowing off a tire, causing the truck to careen to a halt. As machine gun bullets raked the cab, Christopher, before abandoning the vehicle, yelled "Contact" three times into his radio to alert the rest of the convoy. As they leaped into the ditch, a five-ton trailer truck hit the mine field, crashing to a halt at the side of the road. A third truck tried to race through the kill zone but hit the remaining mines. Losing the front wheels of the truck, the driver fought to control his rig as his cargo of high-explosive shells caught fire.

Undaunted, the next truck ran the gauntlet, its driver all too aware that he was carrying a load of noxious chemical gas. Miraculously he made it. The following truck didn't—a rocket smashed into its side—causing it to slew out of control across the road. In less than one minute, the enemy had succeeded in his first objective, blocking the road and halting the convoy in the kill zone.

The lead armored truck, although disabled, continued to attract the enemy's fire. The crew fired back, though the range was so close they doubted whether their grenades fired from the M-79 launcher would have time to arm before hitting the target. A handful of North Vietnamese sappers fought through the driver's fire and crawled over the trucks, planting explosive charges and firing into the huddled drivers in the ditches. The cargoes caught fire and detonated. Gasoline trucks disintegrated into huge mushroom clouds of flame and black smoke. It was these clouds that alerted the American drivers further back down the column on the far side of the rise. From the ditches, individual drivers fired their rifles at the sappers. At such close range they couldn't miss. Enemy soldiers fell from the American trucks like targets at a shooting gallery.

The surviving armored trucks charged into battle. Their machine guns and grenade launchers fought back, trying to suppress the intense enemy fire. A rocket round exploded near a second armored truck. Before its driver could react, another round hit the cab, wounding him. The truck careened out of control, the driver disabled on the floor. The truck hurtled over the edge of an embankment, tossing the crew helplessly about. One man who wasn't flung free was crushed to death when the vehicle overturned.

Gen. Creighton Abrams—spoke admiringly of the gun truckers as "just frustrated tankers."

The four remaining armored trucks maintained the battle. Their firepower kept the convoy from being entirely overrun. The gun trucks fired and moved, using classic armored tactics to save the convoy. After about 15 minutes the enemy withdrew, knowing an American reaction force would soon arrive. The two surviving gun trucks pursued. Their aggressive tactics aroused the compliments of an old armored soldier, General Creighton Abrams, who 23 years earlier, had led his tanks into Bastogne during the Battle of the Bulge in World War Two. The general observed the ambush from a helicopter overhead. After the battle he spoke admiringly of the gun trucks, saying "Those guys are just frustrated tankers."

The gun trucks' gallant conduct was not without cost; four of the six trucks were knocked out. In all, three members of the convoy were killed and 22 wounded, while 13 trucks were totally destroyed and nine damaged. Later a body count determined that the ambushers, a mixed company of Viet Cong and North Vietnamese (VC/NVA) regulars, had sustained 41 dead.

THE FIRING slowly stops. The driver climbs back

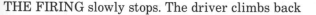

aboard and starts up the engine. Driving over the
crest he sees numerous wrecked trucks, some still
burning. Bodies lie scattered everywhere, but they
are mostly those of the enemy. Dodging through the
wreckage, he worries about puncturing a tire. A rear
tire is OK, since there are two tires side by side. A
front tire is trouble. To maximize carrying capacity
he carries no spare tires. A flat in the front means
he will have to wait for help while the rest of the
convoy drives on.

The convoy arrives at Pleiku. The smaller trucks
unload while the five-ton tractors unhitch their

Ambush!
Ambush!

AMBUSH ALLEY:
A convoy
regroups on
the road from
An Khe to
Pleiku. Dubbed
"Ambush
Alley" because
of the
frequency of
enemy attacks,
it led to the
ratio of gun
trucks to
regular trucks
being
increased
one-to-ten.

trailers and pick up empties. Some of the luckier drivers eat hamburgers and drink cokes while they wait. Others eat the less desirable C-rations, swilled down with tepid water.

Still, the scene is not too different from a truck stop back home. Then it's back into the cab for the return trip. Passing the ambush site there is little to show where there had been fighting. The last wreck is being loaded onto a flatbed truck.

Back at base the driver turns in his log book, showers, eats, and goes to bed. A new convoy will repeat the trip the next day.

The Big Sweeps

1966 HAD been a year of preparation. While new units arrived, an immense nationwide logistical base had been built to support combat operations. This network of service, rest, support, communications, and supply bases dotted the countryside. It had its advantages and disadvantages.

On the plus side, no combat soldier ever had quicker access to superb medical care. Yet the very existence of such care meant that many combat operations would halt while helicopter evacuation of the wounded took place. The VC/NVA noted this American passion for immediately going to the aid of the wounded. Snipers would shoot to wound in order to draw more Americans into a kill zone. At other times, enemy forces conducting rear-guard actions would seek to inflict just enough punishment to cause a unit to halt its pursuit while it looked for a helicopter landing zone to fly out the injured.

Furthermore, American officers boasted how they had at their fingertips more firepower than any soldiers in history. This was absolutely true. The US combat soldier, and armor soldiers in particular, possessed stunning amounts of firepower.

They used it lavishly in such operations as "recon by fire"—shooting up the bush in case someone was there; the "mad minute"—every weapon firing out from a defensive perimeter on full automatic at dusk or dawn in case the enemy was massing for an attack; "interdiction and harassment fire"—blindly shelling various map coordinates to impede potential enemy movement; and "thunder runs"—driving down a road full tilt, firing madly out at the bush to disrupt potential ambushes and mining operations. These tactics, and a host of others, used up amazing amounts of ammunition. While striving to

51

Creature comforts—a war weary receives his scoop of ice cream in the chow line. In the 100° heat it was appreciated. The logistics of supplying US forces required that for every three men at the front, there were two in the rear echelon keeping supply lines open.

limit casualties the American Army wisely tried to substitute firepower for naked valor. However, massive reliance upon firepower carried some hidden costs. At the level of small tactics, APCs were so packed with extra ammunition that soldiers couldn't ride inside of them even if they wanted. On a larger scale, "casualties were taken while loading, unloading, transporting, and protecting the massive amounts of ammunitions required for such prodigious firepower." Many armored units spent most of their service repeatedly clearing roads from one base to another so munitions and supplies could be moved. Such operations kept them from acting aggressively against the enemy.

In addition, the combat soldier became dependent upon a tremendous diversity of "creature comforts." Aerial delivery of ice cream or beer on a regular schedule, even during combat operations, became commonplace. In one mech battalion, the commander would designate someone to go to base each week to buy crates and crates of soft drinks. Each APC would load up, often carrying the drinks in special travel containers normally used to carry whole blood. In the field the only thing lacking was ice. The unit arranged for giant Chinook helicopters to deliver the ice each day.

These luxuries were good for morale, but oversupplied soldiers tended to be very careless. The VC/NVA gleaned remarkable amounts of usable military equipment from American trash heaps. Discarded and dud munitions were gutted to make mines. The explosives were placed in empty American ration containers, powered by discarded American batteries that sent a pulse through salvaged American communication wire. Not until after the war would America learn how much the VC/NVA relied upon American supplies.

Finally, there was a morale cost in excessive reliance upon an elaborate supply system. Obviously, there was the danger the soldiers would grow "soft." But even keen soldiers experienced anger and shock over American habits. One armor trooper recalls how he hated the helicopter ice cream delivery during jungle operations because such deliveries invariably preceded a mortar bombardment the next morning. The observant enemy had accurately located the cavalry's position by watching this resupply effort. Another mech infantry soldier remembers flying into a hot landing zone, taking multiple hits, and then watching the pilot barely manage to fly the crippled chopper full of wounded to a nearby American base. As the bird staggered in for a crash landing, the soldier looked down and saw infantrymen lounging around a fine concrete pool, drinking beer and floating in lounge chairs in the warm water. It was a strange war.

The character of the American fighting soldier gradually changed over time. As the army expanded, increasing numbers of draftees filled the ranks. Some units tried to maintain the same spit-and-polish attitudes that characterized the regular army in peacetime. Often the young draftees put up considerable resistance. Other units took a more

"I'LL SEE THOSE 155S AND RAISE YOU TWO F-8S"

155mm artillery

F-8 Crusader

Political turmoil plagued ARVN armor operations during 1966. Near Da Nang in April the crack 1st ARVN Division joined antigovernment forces in a virtual mutiny. A dissident mechanized column was bombed by South Vietnamese planes, an act that infuriated Americans since the aircraft had used the vital Marine airstrip to stage their bombing runs. As the mutineers approached the base a Marine Corps truck blocked the column on a narrow bridge to prevent it getting within artillery range. In response the ARVN force deployed its 155mm artillery and began to break out ammunition. The commander received word that if he fired on the airstrip he would endanger Americans and that the US forces would fire back.

Nonetheless the Harvard-educated ARVN colonel, who spoke excellent English, radioed to the Marine jets that he was preparing to fire. The Marine Corps pilot responded: "I'll see those 155s and raise you two F-8s." As the jets swooped low and the approaching Marine Ontos took aim the ARVN gunners realized that their bluff was called and folded by elevating their tubes skyward.

accommodating attitude. Thus the staff of the American Division's cavalry squadron referred to one armored group as "the Jesus troop." The troopers' flowing hair spilled well down their backs, reminding the staff of a group of biblical figures. At base this platoon raised a considerable amount of hell. However, when orders came to take to the field, the "Jesus troop" became excellent combat soldiers. An officer recalls that whenever the troop roared out

The Big Sweeps

THUNDER RUN: Tanks of the 1st Marine Division raising dust on an early morning road sweep. The crews expected trouble. The sign on the right of the road as they left camp read: AMBUSH ROW (Last ambush 8 days ago). As the chalked-in figure indicating the number of days since the last ambush increased, so did the tension among the crews detailed for convoy escort duty. The higher the number, the more the likelihood of an enemy attack.

of camp on their way to a new mission, each track sported an American flag. These troopers looked a little different, but their fighting spirit and patriotism was comparable to that of any American cavalrymen throughout history.

The initiative remained in the hands of the VC/NVA during 1966. Operational reports revealed that 88 percent of all fights were begun by the enemy. Almost half of these were ambushes involv-

55

ing infantry. Sixty-three percent of all encounters were against an opponent sheltered in bunkers and fortified trenches.

Beginning in 1967, American commanders hoped to change all of this. Using forces that had arrived during 1966, the Allies could field a formidable army to knock the VC/NVA off balance. Included in this force was a growing armored contingent: the 11th Armored Cavalry; several troops of the 17th Cavalry assigned to light infantry and airborne brigades; divisional cavalry squadrons including the 1/4 Cav, 3/4 Cav, and 1/10 Cav; seven mechanized battalions serving in various infantry divisions; two tank battalions and an independent tank company; and the considerable armored assets of the Marine Corps. The crack 1st Australian Task Force, which included an APC Troop, was available. Ten ARVN Armored Cavalry Squadrons had been created.

Together, these armored units would spearhead the campaign. It was to be the year of the big sweeps and search-and-destroy operations as the Americans sought out mainforce enemy combat units—the year of the big battles when they frequently succeeded in finding the enemy.

THE VERY name of the objective, the "Iron Triangle," carried with it a feeling of dread. Located in an area only 12 miles from Saigon, the Iron Triangle appeared to allied strategists as a dagger pointed at the capital. It was a heavily fortified sanctuary that gave the VC a staging area from which to dominate adjacent population and transportation centers. The allied high command planned to eradicate this menace as part of the strategy to force the enemy away from Vietnamese population centers.

Planning called for the Iron Triangle to be surrounded by allied forces during the first phase of the operation. It was to be the first corps-sized operation involving both American and ARVN forces. Mechanized forces played a key role. From a distant base area, the 11th Armored Cavalry (Blackhorse Regiment) had to drive 60 miles to assume its blocking position along the eastern edge of the triangle. Simultaneously, mechanized elements of the 25th Division would lead a drive against the northern edge. Strategists hoped that the combination of rapid

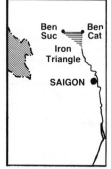

Location of the Iron Triangle 12 miles to the northwest of Saigon. It was here that US forces staged Operation Cedar Falls. It was part of the second phase of the strategy that took the war into enemy strongholds.

armor and helicopter movement would seal off the Iron Triangle before the enemy had time to react. For three days, through January 5 - 8, 1967, various blocking forces took up their positions.

On January 9, spearheaded by tanks and M-113s, US forces penetrated into the Iron Triangle. Expectations exceeded the event. At 8 A.M., the Blackhorse attacked the VC sanctuary. Two hours later they had reached the far side after encountering very slight resistance. Frustrated, American troops began to close in on supposed enemy positions from several directions. Somehow the enemy had escaped.

A tanker recalls that he "felt like I was in the old West in the days of the cavalry and Indians. We were the cavalry. We move around, patrol and patrol, and don't see anything. But they are out there and they know where we are. They will only engage at a time of their choosing."

Despite the lack of contact there were obvious signs that the area had been an enemy stonghold, and to deny the VC future use of the Iron Triangle, a variety of land-clearing techniques were tried. Defoliants rained down from airplanes. Engineers using huge plows hacked away at the jungle. Flamethrowers mounted on M-113s were used to burn away jungle growth from suspected enemy positions. But the 1/4 Cav found that 2,600 gallons of diesel fuel, 1,500 gallons of gasoline, and 1,500 pounds of chemicals were needed to clear a 200-yard long stretch of jungle. This proved an expense that even the American Army could not afford. An alternative had to be found.

During Operation Cedar Falls a partial, and typically American, solution to this problem arose: the so-called "Rome plow" operations. Simply stated, giant armored bulldozers would plow up the jungle to deny cover and concealment to the enemy.

The idea originated from a discussion between General Westmoreland and an acquaintance who had experience clearing land in Australia. While the Australian technique did not work in Vietnam, Westmoreland's interest did prompt a search for a better technique. This led to the Rome K/G Clearing Blade or Rome plow. Named after the city in Georgia where it was manufactured, the plow consisted of a tractor attachment with a blade whose

The 11th Armored Cavalry, better known as "The Blackhorse Regiment," was the first armored squadron to serve in Vietnam.
In the early part of the war it served in Tay Ninh province in War Zone C close to the Cambodian border.
In 1969 it was one of the units chosen to take part in the sweep into Cambodia.

cutting edge sheared small- to medium-diameter
trees off at ground level. A wedgelike projection on
the left side would be used to weaken large trees so
the cutting edge could fell them. In contrast to a
bulldozer, the Rome plow cut through obstacles
instead of digging them out. Heavy steel cabs
protected the operator while a wire mesh provided
overhead protection from falling limbs.

One operator in the Blackhorse Regiment,
Specialist 4 Brett Miller, proudly boasted that
"There is nothing the thing can't go through."
Wielded by an experienced driver, the plow could
move through jungle, toppling everything in its way,
at a faster pace than a running man. Operating
these powerful machines appealed to a certain breed
of man who enjoyed working with heavy equipment.
As Miller explained: "I love it. It's big and I like to

The Big Sweeps

FIELD OF FIRE: Modified M-113 ''Zippo Reb'' of 1/4 Cav uses a flame thrower to burn out antipersonnel mines near Cau Dat during Operation Cedar Falls. The battalion discovered that it took over 2,600 gallons of diesel fuel, 1,500 gallons of gasoline, and 1,500 pounds of defoliant chemicals to clear a 200 yard square of jungle — an extravagant use of materials that even the US Army could ill afford.

drive big equipment. I think everyone, when he was a kid, wanted to operate some heavy equipment. Well, I got that wish.''

In one 56-day operation, a land-clearing team from the 25th Division, protected by the 4/23 Mechanized Battalion, cleared some 12,000 acres of dense jungle. The operation proceeded slowly because the dozers kept uncovering enemy earthworks. Extensively booby-trapped, the area was honeycombed with trenches, bunkers, and tunnels including one multi-level tunnel complex, descending through four levels and extending almost one mile.

Almost every armored unit at some time participated in Rome plow operations. Such a system, with its enormous use of ammunition, fuel, and mechanical equipment, could never have been developed by any but the American Army. Faced with the problem of dense jungle that could hide the enemy, the American Army used raw mechanical power to change the jungle to cleared land. Yet this approach successfully denied the NVA valuable sanctuary areas.

'WAR ZONE C' carried with it the same evil reputation as the Iron Triangle. It occupied a flat, marshy corner of Vietnam along the Cambodian border northwest of Saigon. Like the Iron Triangle, it had been communist-dominated since the formation of South Vietnam. It too served as a vast base area from which to launch attacks against important targets. Somewhere within its confines, intelligence believed, the VC/NVA headquarters (COSVN) for all military operations in the south were located.

During Cedar Falls, the planned barrier formed by blocking troops had proven sievelike. Much of the blame was directed against ARVN forces. This time, Junction City would be a virtually all-American show. Over two divisions would form a giant horseshoe around War Zone C. Once they were in position, the 11th Armored Cavalry and 2d Brigade, 25th Division would be "pitched" into the middle. Unlike a similar plan against the Iron Triangle, Junction City would produce some very serious fighting.

On February 22, 1967, Junction City began in dramatic fashion with a combat parachute jump of elements of the 173d Airborne Brigade. The next day the Blackhorse and 2d Brigade entered the enemy sanctuary. At first it seemed all too much like Cedar Falls. For day after day careful searches were conducted and increasing amounts of war supplies uncovered, but few contacts with fighting men occurred.

Then on March 10 the nature of Operation Cedar Falls violently changed as a heavy attack exploded from the jungle against a base at Prek Klok.

At dusk, the 2d Battalion (Mechanized), 2d Infantry occupied fighting positions surrounding a new base that was under construction. Every 50 yards, all the way around the perimeter, the unit's APCs were placed. In between lay foxholes manned by infantry, artillerymen, and engineers. As the sun went down, the Americans fired off a "mad minute" (all weapons shooting as rapidly as possible into the sur-

The area for Operation Junction City. Unlike Cedar Falls, this was to be an all-American show.

rounding jungle in case the enemy was present). Around 8.30 P.M., outlying listening posts reported enemy movement. The defenders went on alert while preplanned harassing fire from artillery bombarded possible VC lines of approach. Amid increasing tension, an hour and one-half went by. At 10 P.M., a furious bombardment of mortar, recoilless rifle, and rocket propelled grenades (RPGs) deluged the perimeter. Several tracks were hit and some 20 defenders wounded. Cooks and maintenance crews carried the wounded to a small airstrip in the middle of the perimeter where helicopters arrived to fly them to safety.

After 30 minutes the bombardment ceased. Lieutenant Colonel Edward Collins ordered his men to fire again into the jungle in case enemy attackers were massing. No sooner had this ended than some two battalions of enemy troops assaulted the eastern side of the perimeter. Supporting attacks came from other directions. Intrepid VC who had crawled forward undetected to within 25 yards fired RPG rounds that exploded against the armor of three M-113s. Another track received an unlucky blow from a mortar round. On the attackers came.

Their massed ranks crumpled against the defenders' fire. Armored battalions packed an incredible punch with their numerous machine guns. These weapons ripped the attackers apart. Driven

RECON BY FIRE:
Troops of the Blackhorse stage reconnaissance by fire.
This crude but effective tactic was used by armored troops advancing into unexplored territory. It involved indiscriminately deluging a designated target area with rifle and machine gun fire to flush out hidden enemy forces.

back, the VC tried again. Now, however, both artillery and air support were available for the defenders. The enemy were pelted while forming up and annihilated when they tried to charge across open ground against American machine guns. It was a slaughter.

At dawn the Viet Cong broke contact. At the cost of three dead and 38 wounded, the defenders had easily held their ground while inflicting nearly 200 dead on the attackers. Still, such was the discipline of the enemy force that they managed to carry off the weapons of their fallen in spite of the awesome American bombardment. Only 12 individual weapons remained behind.

The Big Sweeps

FLATTENING THE TRIANGLE:
Aerial view of the 80-yard-wide avenues either side of Route 13 ripped out by Rome plows to deny the enemy the sanctuary and create free fire zones. Nicknamed "hogjaws," the 60-ton armored plows were fitted with specially hardened blades that could splinter trees up to three feet in diameter. The "headache" bar above the driver's cab protected him from falling debris. During Cedar Falls, Rome plows changed the face of the Iron Triangle, flattening eleven square kilometers.

After the war, American officers wondered why the VC/NVA threw away their men and material in such attacks. Light infantry fighting armor set in a defensive position supported by artillery and air power never succeeded in overrunning an American base. Yet while trying, they suffered horrible losses. Given the difficulty of infiltrating men and material down from the north in the face of aerial bombardment, famine, and disease, why did the enemy high command so heedlessly throw away their resources? Probably they blundered. Perhaps they persisted because they came close to victory more than once. An example came nine nights later.

After the combat at Prek Klok, Junction City's

search-and-destroy operations expanded. To support these operations a series of fortified bases were built to protect the big guns of the artillery. One such base was located near the small village of Ap Bau Bang. Its garrison consisted of Troop A, 3d Squadron, 5th Cavalry.

The recently arrived 3/5 Cav (Black Knights) served as the recon squadron for the 9th Infantry Division. It was part of the ongoing buildup of American forces taking place during 1967. Although having arrived a mere month ago, the unit had a famous history involving Indian-fighting against almost all the western tribes, from Comanches to Apaches. Its forebears would have felt at home in the "Indian" warfare of Vietnam, particularly on the night of March 20 when Troop A's six tanks and 23 tracks formed a "wagon wheel" defensive perimeter and prepared to meet an attack from any direction.

The perimeter lay surrounded by jungle on three sides and a rubber plantation on a fourth. At 10.30 P.M., a sound that would have been more familiar to troopers serving in the Old West than those in Vietnam alerted the Black Knights. A small herd of cattle came ambling to within 150 yards of the perimeter. Apparently the VC drove these animals toward the Americans in hopes of forcing the defenders to reveal their positions. In any event, this peculiar ruse didn't work. Ten silent minutes followed.

Troop A was was just starting to think that it was a false alarm when a machine gun opened fire from a nearby rail embankment. Specialist 4 Eugene Stevens trained his tank's searchlight on the VC position. Under this illumination, the tank and three tracks fired all weapons for a steady three minutes until the enemy gun fell silent. Another lull ensued during which tankers anxiously scanned the perimeter with infrared optical equipment. Just after midnight the Viet Cong attacked in earnest.

A tremendous barrage of mortar, RPG, rocket, and recoilless rifle fire saturated the Black Knights' position. The accurate fire hit three tracks, causing one to burn, and two tanks. The defenders ducked low awaiting the inevitable infantry assault. Massed troops of the 273d Viet Cong Regiment emerged from the rubber plantation and swarmed across the open ground toward the cavalrymen. From the op-

Unit insignia of the Black Knights —once an Indian-fighting outfit, the unit initially saw Vietnam action at Ap Bau Bang. Later it would be deployed to the northern-most I Corps Tactical Zone to be stationed along the Laotian border.

posite direction a secondary attack rolled toward the Americans.

Captain Raoul Alcala confidently radioed that his troop could handle these attacks. Mortars illuminated the battlefield with flares. The captain could see waves of Viet Cong sweeping toward him. In the front line another tank was struck repeatedly. A defender recalls: "I got two hits on top of my turret from the 60mm mortar rounds, two rounds struck the gun shield below the gun tube. Another round hit the main gun's blast deflector, so we opened fire with everything we could lay our hands on." Here the sturdy value of the Patton tank became apparent. Lighter armor or infantry alone might have succumbed to such fire. The tank shed the hits and continued to function as a powerful fighting vehicle.

However, the VC braved the intense American fire to close on the APCs manning the defensive perimeter. Over the radio of his M-48, Staff Sergeant Dorren heard: "They are swarming all over my track. Dust me with canister." The sergeant hesitated, fearing to inflict damage on his own men. Through the flickering flare light he saw shadowy figures milling around the tracks with wild streams of fire shooting out in all directions, the distinctive green trails of the RPG and AK47 rounds contrasting with the colors left by the American ammunition. "My people are down, shoot!" came the same voice. Desperate, Dorren fired, blowing the figures off the nearby APC. Another track commander called for the same treatment. This time Dorren unhesitatingly complied. The third time did not prove the charm. As Dorren's gun fired on Track 10, the vehicle received several direct hits from mortars and burst into flame. The wounded crew escaped amid enemy shelling that was hitting VC and Americans alike.

The fierce enemy assault forced the Americans to pull back some 25 yards. Front-line foxholes were overrun. The attackers swarmed over immobilized tracks to begin to salvage their weapons. Around this time three more tracks were hit. While the perimeter was holding, the cavalry were taking a frightful battering. They needed help.

Reinforcements arrived from several directions. Although one column had to blast through an ambush to reach Troop A, they arrived in time to

A Xenon searchlight — fitted to an M-48 tank it proved invaluable in nighttime actions. Its high-powered beam could be switched instantly to infrared to illuminate enemy soldiers up to 300 yards away. The introduction of night sights and powerful searchlights slowly altered the attitude once common among US troops that "the night belonged to Charlie."

Location of Ap Bau Bang on Route 13 where armored forces fought a classic defensive action

launch a limited counterattack that pushed the perimeter out some 40 yards and ensured the base's survival.

As dawn approached, helicopters arrived to evacuate the most seriously injured defenders. Many of the lightly wounded troopers chose to remain at their positions and continue to man their weapons. Supported by 29 tons of bombs and 3,000 artillery rounds, a small armored force again proved they could survive in an isolated position. Although they lost three killed and 63 wounded (about one in four defenders had been hit by enemy fire) the Black Knights had administered a costly repulse to the 273d VC Regiment. As was typical in such nighttime defenses, artillery and air power had proved the major killer of the attacking troops. The armor protected the defenders from intense hostile fire while the vehicles' weapons kept the attackers at bay. This gave the guns and jets an opportunity to deliver their lethal hardware against massed enemy formations.

AN EXAMPLE of what could happen to a defensive perimeter lacking armor support came the next night. Fire Support Base Gold was in almost every way like the base near Ap Bau Bang. It lay surrounded by jungle, and its defending company of infantry closely approximated the number of defenders at Ap Bau Bang, yet it was all but overrun by massed enemy infantry before the 2nd Battalion 34th Armor arrived at the spearhead of a rescue column. In contrast to the armored defense of Ap Bau Bang the infantry lost a staggering total of 31 killed and 109 wounded.

This action concluded armor's combat participation in Operation Junction City. The operation was one of the finest military achievements of the war. Tremendous damage was inflicted on the 9th VC Division at an acceptable cost. "Corps-sized Army forces had demonstrated their ability to mass and use great mobility in tackling any area of Vietnam. However...the mobile shock power of such a colossal effort was rarely repeated." Armor had provided much of this "mobile shock power". While constantly at the forefront of Junction City, only three tanks and 21 APCs had been destroyed. With each passing campaign, armor was proving its worth.

On the down side, Junction City presented a perplexing problem. Massive American force had been applied. Yet, while the enemy had been temporarily shattered, the purpose of the big battles of 1967 was to force the VC/NVA into a "vulnerable posture". Instead, the 9th VC Division simply had been forced back into Cambodia. For political reasons, there they were permitted to refit and regroup in peace.

So the pattern of even the largest search-and-destroy operations became apparent. As a veteran of armored combat in both World War II and Vietnam observed, in World War II soldiers knew that each mile of advance brought them closer to Germany. Capturing strategic terrain opened the way. Soldiers could see how their sacrifices brought the end of the war closer. In Vietnam there were no such objectives. An area could be swept, the enemy driven out, bases destroyed, and all too soon the entire effort would have to be repeated. Soldiers could ably perform a monotonous, difficult, dangerous sweep, only to have to repeat it again and again.

**LUCKY DAY:
Troopers of
11th Armored
Cav with
their lucky
horsehoe.
This M-113 had
just been
disabled by a
mine without
incurring
casualties. It
was partly
good luck but
also due to
riding on top of
the vehicle in
direct disregard
of high
command
directives.**

67

Tanks to the Rescue

The Tet Offensive

DURING 1967, the year of the big battles, armor had demonstrated its worth in countless combats. Its value was underscored by the release of a formal evaluation of armor in Vietnam. The study's basic conclusion was that "armor-mechanized units and their equipment enjoy a much greater utility in Vietnam than many thought possible." But the study seemed to have little impact. Skeptics remained, particularly among new officers fresh in for their six-month field commands.

Even in the field, attitudes toward armor varied. A lieutenant in a cavalry squadron who was a self-proclaimed "firepower guy," "loved" operating with tanks because they provided instant artillery support. Yet a battalion commander in a mechanized infantry unit "hated" tanks teaming up with his APCs. He felt that the tanks were always throwing tracks or becoming bogged down and acting as a drag on his battalion's mobility.

To be effective, armor had to remain mobile. Keeping a 52-ton machine running required handyman skills coupled with brute strength. When a tank threw a track or received track damage from mines, the crew would replace any damaged portions of tread. Each tread block weighed 70 pounds. Tools for the job were two types of socket wrenches, a sledgehammer, and a long crowbar known as a tanker's bar. It served as a lever to lift and pry. The sledgehammer freed frozen nuts and encrusted mud. The wrenches tightened the tread.

If a tank was operating close to a base when it lost its track, a truck would deliver a pallet full of replacement treads. Then the truckers would hastily depart, leaving the tankers to their own resources. The tread would be assembled next to the tank,

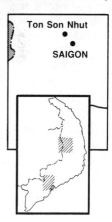

Tanks to the Rescue

BATTLEFIELD REPAIR: Engineers of a 1st Cav armor recovery crew fix a steel hauser from their M-88 tow vehicle (left) to a bogged down M-48. Nearby an M-113 stands guard. To gain traction when towing a nine-ton M-48 out of thick mud, the repair crew lowered the M-88's curved bulldozer blade flat until it anchored in the ground.

placed under a road wheel, and lifted up to the sprocket. Guided by hand signals since voices couldn't be heard over the roar of the engine, the driver would gently race the engine while in neutral. This turned the sprocket, which engaged the new tread and propelled it forward along the support rollers running the length of the tank. One tanker reckons the ancient Eygptians would have been comfortable trying to repair tracks since the mechanical principles and the tools were the same as those used to build the pyramids.

The army's manuals stressed safety while performing these potentially dangerous repairs in

he field men needed to hurry. The dangers con-
fronting a broken-down tank as the sun set and the
jungle seemed to close in haunted many tankers.
Done right by a skilled and brawny crew, the job
took four hours. Done wrong, the entire tread wrap-
ped around the sprocket wheel, leaving the vehicle
a stranded target for the enemy.

At night it was worse. Heavy mechanical labor
meant creating light and noise. One tanker recalls
fixing the track using flare lights shot on command
into the dark sky by friendly mortars. There was no
way the enemy could fail to see what was going on.
However, just in case, the din of hammers striking

The M-107 self-propelled 175mm gun. Despite its ability to fire a shell equivalent in weight to an average-sized man over 20 miles, the 175mm failed to live up to high-command expectations because of short tube life. The 25-foot gun tubes had to replaced after firing just 300 of their 174lb. shells.

metal sent a clear message: "Here we are." Given all of this, it is easy to understand why some armor officers viewed tanks as a burden. It is even easier to understand why some nonarmor officers thought all armor vehicles were a hindrance.

AS AMERICAN generals looked at their strategic maps in the beginning of 1968, their attention was riveted on the northernmost provinces bordering the so-called demilitarized zone (DMZ) that separated North and South Vietnam. A tremendous amount of available military resources were positioned there in the I Corps zone. A series of fortified Marine Corps posts stood in seeming isolation along the DMZ. The high command feared a major assault across the border, and from Laos, might turn one of these bases into a Dien Bien Phu.

Distracted by the threat in the north, US high command seriously underestimated the enemy's potential for major nationwide attacks. As January progressed, disquieting signs of enemy buildup were analyzed, prompting countermeasures.

Early in January, the 4th Division moved a tank company to Pleiku in the Central Highlands to be ready for any unexpected enemy move. Similarly, a few days later General Westmoreland ordered a squadron of armored assault vehicles of the 4th Cavalry to be posted near Saigon's Tan Son Nhut air base. His reckoning was that "they would provide a ready mobile reserve with impressive firepower."

The combination of intelligence reports and a series of premature attacks in the Central Highlands warned the allies of the likelihood of an enemy offensive. Heedless, the South Vietnamese prepared to celebrate their lunar new year. A nationwide ceasefire had been agreed upon by all combatants. The celebration's peak would come the night of January 30.

During the day, Westmoreland's headquarters sent out a warning directing that "troops will be placed on maximum alert with particular attention to the defense of headquarters complexes, logistical installations, airfields, population centers and billets." That evening the decisive Tet Offensive began in earnest. Its violence achieved a surprise similar to the great German attack at the Battle of the Bulge in World War II.

Just as the high command had been in 1944, Saigon seemed aloof from the real war. That night, partiers swarmed the street to greet the New Year. The ban on fireworks had been lifted, so thousands of traditional firecrackers rocked the air. Slowly, as Viet Cong assault forces moved into position, this sound was replaced by the sounds of combat.

One important VC target was the ARVN Armored Command headquarters. Specially trained personnel accompanied the assault to man the vehicles that normally were stationed at this headquarters. If the audacious plan succeeded, the Viet Cong would have tanks and other mechanized equipment to roam the streets of Saigon. By the early morning, ARVN Armored Command headquarters lay in the hands of the Viet Cong. Fortunately its armored vehicles had been removed two months earlier.

Despite being foiled here, the VC attack continued to gain momentum. The US 199th Infantry Brigade

NO IMMUNITY: **Muscles and crowbars straining, a 25th Division tank repair crew prove that no one is immune to mishap as they replace a thrown track on their stranded M-88 tank recovery vehicle stuck in the mud at Cu Chi.**

Saigon and environs — scene of some of the heaviest fighting during the Tet Offensive.

barely managed to cling onto the huge Long Binh supply complex outside of Saigon. At 8 A.M., eight tracks from the reconnaissance troop sped downtown toward the enemy-held Phu Tho racetrack. Heavy automatic weapons fire opened up from the rooftop six blocks from the objective. As the tracks carefully crept forward a rocket crashed into the lead vehicle killing the platoon leader and two crewmen. Hordes of fleeing civilians raced past the stalled column as the troop tried to engage the enemy while evacuating their wounded. Although reinforced, it took five hours to advance two blocks.

The next day the 5th Battalion, 60th Infantry (Mechanized) arrived to help. They quickly found

Tanks to the Rescue

STREET FIGHT: Military Police and infantry take cover behind the MP's Commando V-100 armored car as they advance cautiously down a body-strewn Saigon alley during the street fighting that erupted on January 31, the first day of the Tet Offensive. The alley was at the rear of US Bachelor Officer Quarters in Saigon, a frequent target of surprise Viet Cong attacks.

hat armor operating in narrow streets provided a highly vulnerable target to point-blank machine gun and rocket fire. For several days the fight around he racetrack ebbed and flowed as the American public watched on TV the seeming destruction of Saigon.

On the city's outskirts and throughout the country, armor provided a quick reaction force that staved off many disasters. The Blackhorse Regiment made a 12-hour forced march to Long Binh to help secure this vital base. At nearby Bien Hoa air base, APCs from the 2d Battalion, 47 Infantry (Mechanized) broke through roadblocks and ambushes to counterattack across the runway. In the Saigon

TAKING COVER:
Infantrymen carry a wounded comrade behind the sheltering bulk of an M-113 during house-to-house fighting south of Saigon's Y Bridge. APC Connie "The Pink Pussy Cat" included in its claws a recoilless anti-tank rifle mounted behind the main gunshield while its standard issue .50 cal. machine gun was mounted to the side.

area, the most dramatic intervention came from the 3/4 Cav.

Saigon's major airfield, Tan Son Nhut, was under serious attack. All ARVN reserves had been committed elsewhere. The call went out to the cavalry Starting at dawn 15 miles away, Troop C raced down a major highway to lend assistance. From a helicopter overhead, the squadron commander directed his men around potential ambushes. Nearing the airport, tanks and tracks crashed into the rear of the Viet Cong position, bowling over the wire fence at Gate 51. By severing the defenders from their supplies, the cavalry performed "the deciding action which defeated the main Viet Cong assault" on the base.

Outside the capital the worst fighting was in the ancient capital of Hue. For 26 days the Marines and a variety of other Allied and American armored and foot units struggled to retake the walled citadel in he city's center. Fighting in the rubble, the Marines advanced through rain and fog to assault one house after another. Supporting the flak-vested grunts in their struggle forward were Patton tanks, sometimes holed in several places. Tank crews, shaken by as many as 15 hits striking their armor, had to be replaced each day.

As had been shown in World War II at Stalingrad, a ruined city's streets were no place for armor. Vehicles lost their ability to maneuver. They had to advance along constricted streets, allowing antitank teams to carefully site their weapons with certainty. The Viet Cong blocked all avenues of advance, pelting the armor with RPGs whenever it appeared, causing losses and occasionally destroying vehicles. When a crew evacuated a stricken vehicle, machine gun fire from nearby rooftops raked their exposed bodies.

To counter these tactics, the Marines brought forward vehicle-mounted flamethrowers. The flamethrowers spurted their fiery tongues against a succession of fortified houses, either driving the Viet Cong off or incinerating them in place. In addition, the swift, peculiar-looking Ontos antitank vehicles scurried from cover to blast enemy-held houses with their six-gun volleys. Accurate direct fire buried the defenders in a heap of rubble. After more than three weeks of such combat, the allies recaptured Hue.

Saigon and Hue were only two of the many places where the surprise enemy attacks struck. From a strictly military standpoint, the attackers had suffered a grievous defeat. It would be four years before they were able to launch another nationwide assault.

Armor had played a key role in preventing the enemy from gaining many of his objectives. Time and time again, armored vehicles had proved their ability to endure intense fire, break through ambushes, and rescue beleaguered defenders. But the cost for all combat units had been high and it was one the public had not been prepared for. In the aftermath of Tet, US combat deaths climbed 56 percent. The weekly number of deaths nearly doubled the figures for the previous year, the so-called year of the big battles.

For the first time, armored equipment losses had been so high that there was a real shortage of

An M-48 tank spraying deadly napalm — during the street fighting in Hue, specially converted flamethrowing vehicles proved invaluable in flushing out the enemy. The flamethrower's most effective distance was 100-150 yards with "rods" (flames) fired in 10-20 second bursts.

Tanks to the Rescue

PILLBOX DUTY: ARVN troops in action during the "mini-Tet" of May 1968 near Saigon's Tan Son Nhut air base fire their M-3 from the cover of the turret of an old M-24 Chaffee tank. It was one of several M-24's relegated to use as a static pillbox around the perimeter of the air base. To improve the field of fire the radio aerial had been removed.

material. Gasoline-powered Patton tanks were pressed into service. Compared to diesel-powered machines, these were much more vulnerable to enemy action. In addition to equipment problems, many experienced crews had become casualties during Tet. They proved harder to replace than the vehicles.

TET MARKED a turning point that only slowly became apparent. It was decisive because the losses suffered by the US forces shocked the American public into realizing the terrible cost that war brought. To soldiers in Vietnam, it was an enormous, painful battle in which they had seen the enemy mauled and badly hurt.

Secretary of State Henry Kissinger —claimed that VC losses during Tet had not been a setback for the enemy. Instead he pressed for US negotiators at the Paris peace talks to seek an honorable end to US involvement.

In May came a second enemy offensive, "mini-Tet." Action centered on Saigon and again armor became involved in difficult urban fighting.

Seven days later, the Paris peace talks began as enemies met over the negotiating table. American leaders failed to completely comprehend the VC/NVA tactic called "fighting and talking." From now on, diplomatic battles in Paris would be intimately connected with combat in Vietnam. In the hope of favorably influencing peace discussions, North Vietnamese generals planned another heavy attack. With so much American strength deployed around Saigon, the enemy saw an opportunity out near the Cambodian border.

Out on the Border

7

Battles along the Ho Chi Minh trail

WHEN AN American infantry platoon ambushed a VC/NVA battalion near Tay Ninh City on August 17, 1968, no one could know that this action would mark the beginning of ten days of intense combat. Later, historians would deem it the "Third Offensive." To the men in the field, it was a small and reasonably successful combat. To their commander it was something more.

The infantry had been part of a "trip wire" operation. By intercepting enemy movements, they provided an early warning of danger. In this case, the combat warned the 1st Brigade of the 25th Infantry Division that large-scale enemy attacks could be expected. Consequently, Lieutenant Colonel Duke Wolf alerted his command to prepare for all eventualities.

Wolf's 1st Brigade went by the name the "Lancers," a throwback to the time when mounted combat meant men on horses armed with sword and lance. The "Lancers" comprised one of the largest collections of armored fighting units in Vietnam. In addition to two-foot battalions (called leg units), it had two mechanized battalions, a small tank battalion, and a battalion of artillery. With a strength of about 2,000 men backed by 1,500 support personnel, the brigade was entrusted with defending seven US bases, keeping open the roads leading to these bases, maintaining offensive operations, and supporting the civilian economy and administration of the province. This was no small responsibility for a fairly small force.

The area of operations covered the notorious "War Zone C, a region 30 miles northwest of Saigon, surrounded on three sides by Cambodia. Throughout the war, the zone had served as a rest and staging

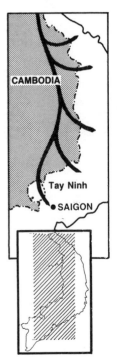

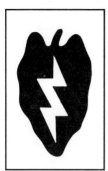

Insignia of the 25th Division— known as the "Tropic Lightning," the Hawaii-based 25th has never served on the US mainland. It earned its now-official nickname from the speed with which it relieved the Marines at Guadalcanal in World War II.

area for enemy troops. Operation Junction City had taken place here. Six months earlier enemy troops had used this route to infiltrate large forces close to Saigon for the Tet offensive. After a second nationwide offensive in May, the so-called mini-Tet, the battered enemy withdrew to the sanctuary offered by this rugged area bordering "neutral" Cambodia. Here, at one of the termini of the network of supply lines running down from North Vietnam that became known as the Ho Chi Minh trail, they could refit and re-equip their forces, knowing that if pressed, they could retreat across the border to safety.

During the Tet and May attacks, the American casualty rate had soared to nearly 500 killed per week. In four months, total American losses had doubled the number of casualties suffered for the previous eight years. Hoping to prevent another devastating psychological victory if the VC/NVA forces penetrated Saigon a third time, American forces had pulled back to the capital area to form a tight defensive perimeter. This action left the 1st Brigade alone, out on the Cambodian border.

The battlefield included open agricultural land, rubber plantations, patches of forest, and jungle. Tracked vehicles could move rapidly on the road network and with reasonable ease through the rubber plantations. However, with the advent of the monsoon season, movement through the rice paddies and jungle was severely restricted.

Taking account of these difficulties Wolf gave the brigade's two infantry battalions largely static assignments. A grunt hefting his basic load through the summer heat fell prey to rapid exhaustion. Therefore, the "leg" units seldom ventured out more than three miles from base. Here they set up their trip wire positions. The leg infantry also provided close-in security to the seven American bases with dug-in positions fortified with wire and mines.

This left active daylight operations in the hands of the mechanized units. The brigade had some 160 armored personnel carriers and 15 M-48 tanks. Each day they left the bases to either search for the enemy or escort convoys. Often such reconnaissances found nothing. The noise of the vehicles thrashing about warned off the VC/NVA. But sometimes their speed surprised enemy formations. Then the mechanized

forces would call in the tremendous American firepower to batter the enemy until he dispersed. Such spoiling attacks were designed to prevent the VC/NVA from massing for night assaults on the American bases.

When the recon units failed to locate sizable enemy units, Colonel Wolf could assume the enemy remained in the rear area sanctuaries along the border. When heavy contacts occurred, the colonel could begin to worry that they were massing for the assault.

The real danger to the bases came at night. At dusk the armored vehicles withdrew into the various fortified perimeters (the bases were surrounded with barbed wire and heavily protected by bunkers and

ROAD SWEEPER: One of the 15 M-48 tanks of the 25th on patrol in War Zone C. Constant road sweeps were standard tactics intended to deter the enemy from massing for night attacks.

M-48 PATTON

Directly descended from the World War II Patton series, the M-48 medium tank was the mainstay of US armor during the Vietnam war. In 1969, the peak year for US involvement, there were some 370 M-48s serving in Vietnam.

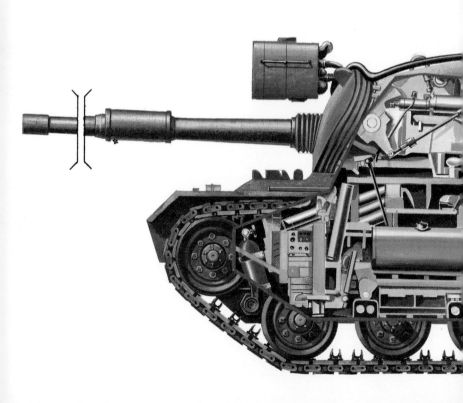

Manned by a crew of four consisting of a commander, a gunner, a loader, and a driver, the M-48 had a top-speed of 30mph. Its armaments consisted of a 90mm gun, a 7.62mm machine gun by the commander's cuppola and a .50 cal. machine gun by the loader's cuppola. The Xenon searchlight above the main gun was an optional extra that could illuminate the enemy up to half a mile away. Heavily armored, the M-48 had a combat load of 47 tons that could crush through thick jungle clearing in 15 minutes to create an LZ for a helicopter.

M-41 A3 WALKER BULLDOG

The standard US Army scout tank of the
50s and early 60s, the M-41 light tank was
supplied to ARVN forces from 1965.
Although its four-man crew quarters were
considered cramped, this did not bother
the physically smaller Vietnamese who
found it rugged and reliable. With a top-
speed of 45mph, a 76mm main gun, and a
7.62 machine gun it was used by ARVN
forces with considerable effect in the late
60s as 'Vietnamisation' began to take
effect and South Vietnamese armor
became responsible for controlling
its own destiny.

trenches). Thus the APCs aided the defense with their machine guns and the tanks with canister-firing 90mm guns.

Outside the wire, small enemy teams would lay mines throughout the province's road network. Or, if more than routine harassment was intended, they would leave their rear area camps and march to a forward assembly area on the edge of War Zone C. Next, they would advance to an attack position in the jungle near the target. If the jungle extended to the edge of the base, this attack position could be well forward. There, the VC/NVA would dig in, lay communication wire, and site supporting weapons.

This period of preparation made the VC/NVA units vulnerable to armored strikes if an aggressive commander was willing to deploy his mobile forces according to good armored doctrine. Colonel Wolf was such an aggressive commander. The problem in this particular case was that there were over 16,000 enemy troops and only 2,000 defenders.

Three hours after an American infantry platoon sprung one such ambush, the VC/NVA Third Offensive began. An entire enemy regiment of over 2,000 men assaulted Fire Support Base Buell. Inside the perimeter stood 400 Americans including a battery of six 155mm self-propelled howitzers, a mechanized infantry company with 17 M-113s, and four M-48 tanks.

Repeated charges crumpled against the defensive perimeter. The American artillery delivered devastating blasts of beehive and timed fuse ammunition. Their defensive barrage was thickened by streams of machinegun fire from the APCs and the infantry. The tanks blasted the attackers at the amazingly close range of 50 yards with canister fire.

Morning came and armored units sortied from the other American bases to intercept the retreating enemy. The majority of the surviving attackers evaded further contact, having suffered heavy losses. The first major assault had been repulsed. Armored fighting vehicles, served by brave men, had again demonstrated what a stout defense they could put up, even when outnumbered five to one. Fighting from the protection of their armored vehicles and the sandbagged shelter of their bunker line, the Americans had suffered three killed and 24 wounded.

A captured VC sapper, stripped to the waist to avoid clothing catching on the razorwire, demonstrates how he cut through the perimeter wire of a US base to lay satchel charges.

That same night, another enemy force—comprising two local Viet Cong battalions—infiltrated into Tay Ninh City, the provincial capital. The local province chief asked for help to drive them out. Colonel Wolf planned to block the VC's retreat with an armored task force from the 2d Battalion, 34th Armor, while the province chief's forces drove the VC against this position. In this way the armored force would serve as the anvil to the hammer of the provincial forces.

To arrive at their assigned position outside Tay Ninh City, Wolf's tankers had to survive an ambush lasting 30 minutes. Meanwhile, a mechanized battalion established its blocking position. When joined by the tanks the anvil was in place.

Unfortunately, the province chief refused to do his part and the hammer never struck. So the Americans attacked into Tay Ninh City alone.

It proved to be a mistake. The enemy skillfully operated from hidden positions in buildings and behind walls. Advancing up the street, the mechanized units could not maneuver. Two leading APCs were hit and destroyed by rocket fire. The American attack was further hampered by high command's prohibition against using mortar, artillery, or air strikes within the city.

This problem quickly intensified when crowds of civilians streamed from a large temple on the city's outskirts. From these crowds, enemy gunners opened fire on the Americans. The mechanized troops returned the fire, killing several innocent civilians. This would later cause an investigation and a severe dress-down for the American troops.

Recognizing that intense street fighting would quickly use up his limited force, Colonel Wolf ordered the attack halted. The Americans killed, according to body count, 42 enemy, but they themselves lost eight killed and 35 wounded.

Fortunately, another American unit appeared on the battlefield, Troop B of the 3rd Squadron, 4th Armored Cavalry. Advancing from the opposite direction, the cavalrymen managed to catch some 200 enemy in the open. This discouraged the VC and they left Tay Ninh that night. Captured documents revealed that the VC had intended to hold the city for three days. American armor had foiled them.

On the third day, August 20, 1968, a remarkable

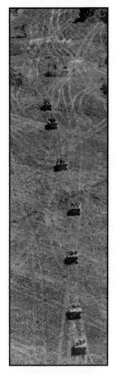

A column of M-113s snakes through the Crescent area near Tay Ninh City after a successful action. Always wary of mines and ambushes, drivers followed in each others' tracks but kept their distance in case the APC ahead should be disabled by enemy fire and block their escape route.

enemy force entered the battle, the 275th VC/NVA Infantry Regiment. Some 75 percent of the regiment comprised North Vietnamese regular army soldiers. No guerrillas, these—the regular soldiers were unmistakable in the field, fighting with helmets, uniforms, and a soldier's normal accoutrements. Combined with the Viet Cong, the composite VC/NVA unit blended local savvy with the discipline and superior equipment of the NVA regular. The 275th was a formidable force.

At ten in the morning, the 275th struck a task force of the 4th Battalion, 23d Mechanized Infantry. Every day this battalion faced the same assignment: clear Highway 13 that led back to Saigon. In the predawn hours, rear area personnel would rise to load their big trucks for the day's run. Leaving at dawn under direction from the military police, the convoy would head toward Tay Ninh, escorted for the first half of the journey by the "Quarterhorse" armored cavalry. The convoy would meet the mech

NIGHT DEFENSE: A well-dug-in M-48 ready for the night. The crew has attached sections of track to the turret to protect against rocket-propelled grenades. The well-prepared earth and sandbag barrier was a common sight at permanent combat bases. Next to the tank is the crew's living quarters. One unofficial innovation was to run a rope from the gun trigger back to the tent so that the crew could fire the first round of beehive before they even reached the tank.

Insignia of the 4th Bn, 23d Mechanized Infantry —on arrival in Vietnam from Alaska the 4/23 served as foot soldiers before being reorganized as a fully mechanized unit in January 1967. Throughout the war the 4/23 served under the command of the 1st Brigade, 25th Infantry Division.

infantry coming from the opposite direction. Then the Quarterhorse would turn back, their duty done.

It was the beginning of the danger time for the 4/23 Mechanized Infantry. Lieutenant Colonel Clifford Neilson and his men knew nothing ever happened in the afternoon. Rather, the enemy would ambush after a night's preparation. Furthermore, they would leave the armor alone on its way to link up with the convoy. They had too much respect for armor's firepower. What they were after was a softer target, the trucks themselves.

So the American convoy advanced along a road through two miles of rubber plantation. French planters had carved these plantations out from the jungle back in their days of colonial occupation. All the underbrush was cleared. Small roads bisected the orderly lines of thick rubber trees. Here was one of the three or four places the enemy habitually struck. To reduce the threat of ambush, rubber trees had been knocked down by Rome plows in a 50-yard strip on either side of the road. But the job hadn't been finished. Heaps of rubber trees still lined the road, offering excellent concealment to the enemy while providing a barrier to off-road vehicle movement. It was, the Chief of Staff of the Australian army, Vietnam, later observed, "a major blunder."

This became apparent when heavy automatic weapons fire and occasional rocket rounds pelted the American vehicles, forcing them to halt. Typically the enemy aimed at a truck at the front and one at the back in order to immobilize the convoy. They chose a place where the escorting APCs couldn't turn back to help out.

The duel continued with each side's machine guns keeping the opponent from closing to decisive range. The Americans called in artillery, mortars, and air strikes, but these seemed to do little more than temporarily reduce the volume of hostile fire. By dusk the Americans recognized it was a stalemate and withdrew into their defensive perimeters for the night.

The next day they returned to find the 275th VC/NVA still entrenched along both sides of the road. The action progressed much as the day before, with the roadbound APCs firing left and right into the rubber plantation against a hidden enemy. Captured documents revealed the enemy plan. The

275th had orders to hold three miles of the road for three days in order to deny use of the road to American supply vehicles. But knowing what the enemy intended did little toward solving the problem of what to do about them.

At noon, from a position about a mile past the far end of the enemy-controlled road, a scouting detachment of the 3d Squadron, 4th Armored Cavalry was ambushed. Once again the enemy concealed himself amid the felled rubber trees. The armored cavalry tried to assault the enemy's entrenchments using M-48 tanks to spearhead the effort. Supported by artillery, air strikes, and helicopter gunships, the attacking Americans struggled forward for six hours.

The 275th skillfully used the terrain to delay the advance, showing "great determination" according to the 1st Brigade commander. In spite of lavish American firepower, the cavalry managed to advance only the length of one football field per hour.

BIG RUBBER:
The rubber plantations northwest of Saigon presented a special challenge. While the small roads that bisected the "Big Rubber" could provide clear fire lanes, the planataion also provided the enemy with staging areas for ambushes.

Out on the Border

AMBUSH PROCEDURE: If the tracks could not keep moving, standard operating procedure was for the infantry to dismount immediately after the ambush was sprung. secured a small defensive perimeter round each M-113 to keep the enemy out of rocket propelled grenade range. A hit from an RPG could turn the M-113's aluminium armor into a funeral pyre —or mean a long walk home.

It was a cruel reward for their effort when they received orders to give up their gains and retire into the defensive perimeter when night fell.

That same day, on another front, a task force of the 1st Battalion, 5th Mechanized Infantry found itself in combat with a sister regiment of the 275th. Probing the jungle edge, the Americans encountered heavy fire from the 33d VC/NVA Regiment.

The 33d swarmed out of the jungle, striving to

engage the APCs at close range. Using tactics
similar to those of the spear carrying Zulus against
the rifle armed British almost 100 years earlier, the
VC/NVA tried to outflank the fighting vehicles using rapid foot movement, and then assault from all
directions. Instead of spears, the VC/NVA's short
ranged weapons were rocket propelled grenades.
They managed to surround one APC, setting it on fire.

Having probed and stirred up a hornet's nest, the

Americans withdrew from the jungle edge into more open terrain. Just as the British formed a square (a defensive formation facing in all directions) when confronted by Zulus, the American armor formed a wagon-train circle to resist the aggressive enemy. Using the machine guns of the APCs, they dueled with the enemy forces, calling in artillery to bombard the treeline. Several times they advanced, only to be driven back. After six hours the VC/NVA broke contact. The Americans lost two killed and 24 wounded in addition to the destroyed M-113.

With night approaching on August 21, Wolf had to evaluate the meaning of the several fierce contacts that had occurred during the day. He felt that the presence of such large enemy forces threatened certain American fire bases. Consequently they would need reinforcements. Before night put an end to all movement, he ordered several small units to move to the endangered posts.

Driving along Route 239 in the fading light, a mechanized infantry company and a recon platoon—a force comprising about 200 men, 17 APCs, and three tanks—hurried toward its assigned position at an American base.

To reduce the mine threat, a tank led the column, hopefully detonating any hidden explosives. In spite of their weariness, the men tried to peer through the gloom of the rubber plantation. Suddenly a hail of

NIGHT LAAGER: Tanks and APCs from the 4/23 "Tomahawks" form a circle for nighttime defense. US armor preferred the open spaces of dried out paddies to the closed in jungle.

small arms fire struck the armor plating. The two front tracks were hit by RPG rounds and caught fire. The men dove for cover. Route 239 was blocked by an enemy ambush that extended for over a mile on both sides of the road. Again, the enemy had used the inadequately cleared rubber trees for concealment. The tanks turned on their searchlights to illuminate the enemy positions. This took courage, since while revealing the enemy, it also clearly marked their own positions. The Americans fired canister from their tanks, blasting the jungle on both sides of the road. The APCs added their machine guns while the infantry contributed rifle fire. Overhead, helicopters tried to support the ambushed column with flares and firepower.

With the road blocked by the wrecked APCs, and off-road movement impeded by the downed trees, the Americans presented a sitting target. The two tanks at the column's rear, pinpointed by their lights, were knocked out by close-range rocket fire. The entire column stood in danger of annihilation.

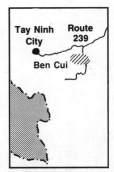

Route 239 to Tay Ninh City —rubber plantations on both sides of the road made it classic ambush territory.

The lead tank saved the force. Amid the fire and confusion, it pushed the wrecked tracks off the road. The column revved its engines and bravely ran the gauntlet of enemy fire. They paid a high price, six killed and 38 wounded, one in four of those engaged, plus four destroyed armored vehicles.

After four days Colonel Wolf's force was seriously depleted. Wolf pleaded with high command for reinforcements but none were sent. Wolf reasoned that if he sat tight, the enemy would move freely and mass in such numbers that they could overrun the bases he had to protect. So he planned on continuing to use the daylight hours to harass the enemy and keep him off balance. He also thought he had to try again to clear Route 26.

Consequently, for the third day in a row, the 4th Battalion, 23d Mechanized Infantry, attacked the enemy roadblock on Route 26. This time the enemy fell back slowly, trading space for time. They destroyed bridges as they retired. To get at the enemy, the battalion employed a tool familiar to tankers in Europe, an armored-vehicle-launched bridge. Instead of having to spend time building a new bridge, a specially modified tank drove to the bridging site and dropped a metal bridge over the water. Thus, the Americans could quickly follow up the retreating

enemy. With the aid of 16 air strikes, the battalion gained ground. But it was ground the enemy willingly yielded, since the 275th VC/NVA Regiment only withdrew after succeeding in its goal of blocking Route 26 for three days.

Meanwhile, in a different area, a small mechanized team probed the Ben Cui rubber plantation, site of the tough fight with the 33d VC/NVA Regiment the day before. The team comprised nine M-113s carrying some 35 soldiers. Operating nearby was

Out on the border

INSTANT BRIDGE: An M-113LAB (Light Assault Bridge) maneuvers into position before laying its folding scissors span across a small river during an operation near Tay Ninh City. Early experience of pursuing an enemy across territory riddled with 3,500 miles of inland waterways quickly proved the need for a fast mobile bridge. The LAB was developed at the specific request of the Army. Based on the M-113 chassis, it had a 30-foot span.

another mechanized unit, a recon platoon. Both units belonged to the 1st Battalion, 5th Mechanized Infantry. As the recon platoon approached a small village at about 10 A.M., it observed hundreds of enemy soldiers rapidly advancing. The platoon radioed this information to the mechanized team and quickly fled. This was the proper thing for them to do—their job was to try to find the enemy. They had done so in a big way.

The mechanized team remained. Its commander

BIG BROTHER: To bridge wider gaps the 60-foot span AVLB (Armored Vehicle Launch Bridge) was used. Built on Chrysler's M-60 tank chassis, it could support the ten-ton weight of a combat-loaded M-113 armored personnel carrier.

recognized that the open ground amid the rubber plantation offered unobstructed fire lanes. Rather than have to fruitlessly seek the enemy in the jungle, he would have them obligingly come to him.

Six APCs deployed forward, with a reserve of three vehicles. For 30 minutes wave after wave of enemy soldiers swept forward into the assault. They fell in heaps before the Americans' machine guns. But some got close enough to fire rocket grenades from their RPG2s and RPG7s. The first tracks burst into flame.

The American commander might have tried to withdraw at this point. By remaining in position, he sacrificed the advantage of his vehicles' mobility. But to have retreated in the face of intense fire would have meant abandoning the men from those vehicles already hit. He chose to stay, and it was a terrible mistake.

The enemy charged again and overran the lead troops, killing all 28 officers and men and destroying their six APCs. The 2d lieutenant who commanded the reserve platoon saw all of this. He was newly arrived in Vietnam and now faced an awful choice: to run for it or to stay and try to help his comrades. He correctly ordered his unit to move out. They easily outdistanced the attacking enemy foot soldiers.

Several mistakes contributed to the disaster at Ben Cui. First, the battalion commander should not have sent out such an understrength unit to probe an area known to contain a large, aggressive enemy force. Where APCs typically carried ten to twelve men, in this unit each carried less than five. Second, the company commander should have used his ability to fire and maneuver. Instead he ordered his unit to halt and engage.

A battalion commander familiar with this incident takes a sympathetic view of the company commander's decisions: once combat began it was not easily apparent which direction to move to escape. Front, flank, and rear become confused when enemy fire strikes from different directions. And there is a kind of unwillingness to abandon a damaged vehicle.

TWO DAYS after the destruction of the American mechanized team, the enemy made another major effort to overwhelm the Lancers. They chose to attack Fire Support Base Buell again. At 1 A.M. on August 24, the assault began. Their tactics were the same as their attack six days earlier, but this time they brought twice the firepower. Undoubtedly, they also relied on the American defenders being tired and worn down by continuous combat.

Their hopes were dashed by deadly point-blank fire from towed and self-propelled artillery pieces firing canister and high-explosive rounds. This fire, combined with tank cannons and the machine guns of the APCs and infantry in their bunkers, halted the attackers before they breached the protective wire.

When the enemy broke contact before dawn they left more than 200 soldiers killed on the ground. The Americans suffered 22 wounded and none killed. It was a spectacular victory.

Two days later, a final series of actions ended the 1st Brigade's participation in this very difficult

Soviet-built Type 69 RPG7 rocket-propelled grenade —introduced in 1962, it proved a significant weapon. Effective up to 500 yards and capable of penetrating armor up to 250mm thick, it proved lethal against the M-113, whose cardboard-thin plating never exceeded 35mm.

campaign. Typically, it began with an ambush. A supply column of close to 100 trucks, laden with ammunition and fuel, was driving toward Tay Ninh City along Route 22.

Along one side of the road, four companies of Viet Cong lay stationed in a six-foot-deep trench. One end of this trench line was secured by a fortified farmhouse, the other by a Buddhist temple. On the opposite side of the road, another VC company manned positions along a straggling village that lay

Out on the Border

JUNGLE BAIT: M-113s from the 25th Inf Div cut through the dense jungle of the Central Highlands during a 1967 operation. By this stage enemy tactics were to lure US forces into remote areas away from the populated lowlands in the hope of inflicting significant military defeats. US forces accepted the bait as part of their "find, fix and finish" policy. They relied on the superior firepower and mobility provided by their APCs and helicopters to never be lured to an area long enough to be endangered.

just off the road. The entire position offered cover and concealment while the two strong points at either end defended the VC from any effort to attack, or "roll up", their flank.

With admirable fire discipline the hidden enemy allowed the first 80 vehicles to pass through the kill zone. There they struck, selecting the rearmost 15 vehicles. Their opening volley knocked out a jeep and a 2.5-ton truck at the front and an ammunition vehicle at the column's rear. In between, trapped,

103

lay 12 vehicles carrying 105mm and 155mm ammunition. The VC prized this load since most of their mines came from American ammo. Clearly, they had good intelligence about the convoy.

Nearby American forces reacted immediately. Here the Lancers' mobility due to their M-113s again proved invaluable. From one end of the ambush, two tracks carrying 11 men sped to the rescue, from the other direction 16 men in four tracks attacked despite the odds against them.

In the event, the two weak platoons made little progress against the two fortified positions at either end of the ambush. In fact, when the enemy recognized how small the reaction force was, they counterattacked, threatening to surround the APCs. The potential for another disaster like that at Ben Cui loomed large when help arrived from overhead.

Colonel Wolf's personal UH-1D Huey helicopter, responding to the convoy's distress messages, swooped down, firing machine guns and dropping several cases of tear gas. The VC withdrew to their fortified position. Even better, Lieutenant Colonel Clemens Riley radioed that Troop B of his 3d Squadron, 4th Armored Cavalry was available to help. Thirty minutes later, Troop B attacked the fortified farmhouse.

Bell "Huey" helicopter— the workhorses of the Vietnam war. Flown by the Army, Navy and Marines, Hueys were used as close air support and command helicopters.

They assaulted with great élan. Facing heavy small arms and RPG fire, a platoon of cavalrymen led personally by the troop commander stormed the VC strong point. The attack succeeded at the price of the commander's life and that of four of his men. Another 11 were wounded. However, the successful assault partially levered the VC out of one end of the mile-long trench.

Simultaneously, a battery of 155mm self-propelled artillery moved into position to lend fire support. Command mix-ups snarled further efforts to organize help for the convoy. Consequently, relatively small US forces continued to try to attack the enemy from outside the ambush zone. Troop B, reduced to about 50 cavalrymen, and Company C, 3d Battalion, 22d Infantry, reduced to a mere 40, valiantly strove to assault the enemy. After 20 minutes they had to give up the effort.

The next day the VC broke contact having lost perhaps 100 dead. American losses were 12 killed and 38 wounded as well as five prime movers and assorted other vehicles. The bulk of the precious ammunition cargo remained in American hands.

The next night the 275th VC/NVA Regiment launched another assault against an American fire support base. But the enemy, too, had wearied during the ten days of combat. Although they penetrated to the wire, they could not make further progress against the American firepower. It was the same story of artillery beehive and firecracker rounds, thickened with machine gun fire from the M-113s, putting up an impassable steel wall. With this final repulse, the Third Offensive in Tay Ninh province came to an end.

Over the ten-day period the enemy failed in most of his tactical goals. The VC/NVA did not seize an American fire support base, nor did they capture Tay Ninh City. Only in the secondary objective of blocking Route 26 for three days had they succeeded. For this they paid a terrible price: some 1,500 killed and probably twice that number wounded.

The ten-day campaign of the 1st Brigade, 25th Division had been a near-run thing. The Lancers lost 81 killed and about 400 wounded, almost 25 percent of its combat soldiers. Much of the danger was down to the high command's fixation with the security of Saigon.

Beyond this major mistake, the campaign revealed other problems. An Australian major general noted that security at all American bases was poor. Local Vietnamese worked on bases and were allowed free passage in and out. This permitted enemy agents to infiltrate and carefully observe the target before attacking. In addition American unwillingness to operate at night limited the possibilities of decisively defeating the enemy. The Australian officer commented: "I could never understand how American commanders could sit behind their defenses and allow an enemy defeated by firepower to drag away their dead and wounded, escape, regroup and live to fight another day." Criticisms aside, although outnumbered eight to one, American forces had successfully defended their bases against a skilled, determined enemy. The mobility of the armored force played a vital role in this. It effectively multiplied American strength, allowing a unit to rapidly maneuver tremendous firepower over large expanses of ground.

An APC maneuvers through the perimeter wire of a fire base for a daytime patrol. But the reluctance of US commanders to commit troops to nighttime pursuit of the enemy drew barbed comment from one foreign obvserver.

Your Motto Is Attack

8

Cavalry actions in Quang Tin

"I EXPECT this cavalry squadron, if it doesn't already have the motto, to adopt that motto of *attack!*" These words greeted the troopers of a cavalry squadron when Brigadier General De Puy of the 1st Infantry Division inspected them on April 15, 1966. For cavalry squadrons serving in Vietnam the general's message was a turning point.

Before Vietnam, every infantry division in the American Army included an armored cavalry squadron. The retention of the term squadron was itself a reminder of that mounted history. In a modern army that hadn't fielded any horse-mounted troops for some 25 years, certain mounted traditions were proudly preserved. Officers who had never seen an old-style cavalry charge would still describe an advance of tracked vehicles carrying soldiers with automatic weapons in such terms as "they drew sabres and charged!" It was part of an esprit de corps the cavalry tried hard to maintain in the jungles and rice paddies of Vietnam.

So, instead of battalion, it was a squadron; instead of company, a troop. Each of the three armored cavalry troops comprised three platoons, the basic maneuver unit. Each platoon, in turn, had a scout section with four ACAVs, a tank section with three Patton tanks, a support squad in a mechanized mortar carrier, a rifle squad and a headquarters vehicle. Thus each platoon packed a formidable amount of firepower.

Conventional wisdom, appropriate for the European battlefield, stated that the divisional armored cavalry squadron's job was to locate the enemy. This scouting role was another throwback to the days of dusty riders of the US cavalry. In theory, once the enemy was located, the main force battalions—

infantry and tanks backed by ample artillery—
would be called in to actually fight the enemy. In
Europe, the cavalry was supposed to use their
mobility to evade heavy engagements while keeping
headquarters informed of the enemy's whereabouts.
This was the historical role of light cavalry since
man invented the stirrup: to find, harass, and
disrupt, while keeping out of major combat. In
Vietnam, the cavalry kept the find, harass, and
disrupt parts of their mission. But they added major
combat to their Vietnam job description. Instead of
merely acting as the army's eyes and ears, once they

Your motto is attack

CAVALRY CHARGE, VIETNAM STYLE: M-113s and M-48s of the 1st Cav move out in line as they go into action on a recon-by-fire mission in the Rice Bowl area. Check the trooper on the rear of the nearest track. The deck chair was to enhance his field of fire —and his comfort.

established contact, they would try to close and destroy the enemy.

The 1st Cavalry had a proud tradition going back to 1833 when it had been organized for the Black Hawk War. It had seen continual service in Mexico, the Civil War, almost every Indian war, and all the way through World War II, when it had formed a regiment of the famous 1st Armored Division. It boasted that it was the most battle-honored unit in the US Army.

In Vietnam the cavalry maintained that illustrious record for front-line valor while developing new combat tactics. This was never better demonstrated than on an August morning in 1968 when Lieutenant Thomas Ginz found himself on a scouting assignment west of Tam Ky, in Quang Tin Province in the I Corps Tactical Zone. Ginz's platoon of the 1st Squadron, 1st Cavalry—together with a troop of South Vietnamese armored cavalry—probed the rice paddies looking for trouble. What they found led to the intense four-day combat at Tam Ky.

Maneuvering along an area of rice paddies and dikes, some ARVN cavalrymen approached a treeline along a gentle rise of ground. Exploding from concealed positions came the too-familiar mix of anti-armor fire; rocket propelled grenades, recoilless rifles, and automatic weapons. A heavily hit ACAV began to burn. The ARVN troop leader called Ginz for help.

As the American tracks moved to provide suppressive fire, the ARVN troopers attempted a bold maneuver, a mounted frontal charge against the enemy high ground. Intense hostile fire drove them back, but not until the troopers had destroyed one 75mm recoilless rifle and captured another.

Shortly after noon, two troops of the 1/1 Cav arrived to help. These reinforcements extended the front of Ginz's embattled platoon. As the Americans spread out looking for the flanks of the enemy's fortified position, they instead found themselves confronted with an impenetrable wall of fire from the enemy-held high ground. Although this gentle rise

BOOTS AND SADDLES: 1/1 Cav ACAVs ready to break camp on operations north of Quang Tin. The folding armored trim vanes are raised to stop water from washing over the hull when fording. They also provided useful storage space for C rations and canvas cots.

lay no more than 30 feet above the rice paddies, firing positions sited there still dominated the open rice paddies. Also, the North Vietnamese position was more extensive than had been supposed.

At one point, Troop A faced extremely heavy fire and was forced to "circle the wagons" in order to fight back in all directions. Captain Christopher Noble recalls that "We were in the circle with the troop when we saw a tank get hit with an RPG round. Four medics were immediately on the spot and found one man with part of his back blown off. The CO (commanding officer) tried calling in a dustoff (medical evacuation helicopter), but before they had a chance to arrive, another chopper descended into the middle of the troop." The squadron commander, Lieutenant Colonel Richard Lawrence, had brought his command and control ship down to rescue the wounded trooper. Inspired by this dramatic intervention, the cavalrymen fought on.

Insignia of the 1st Squadron, 1st Cavalry —motto: Courage and Honor. The 1,000-strong unit was traditionally part of the 1st Regiment of Dragoons. For service in Vietnam it consisted of three ground cavalry troops and one air cavalry troop.

Until now, the cavalrymen had performed their primary task of locating the enemy and developing the situation. Now they began the part of their job unique to Vietnam: closing with the enemy. First, Colonel Lawrence requested reinforcements. An infantry company was promised, so Troop C set off to secure a helicopter landing zone.

As they entered the middle of a small forest, fire erupted from all directions. Again cavalrymen were forced into a tight defensive perimeter with vehicles facing in a 360-degree arc. A track commander explained: "The men never stopped fighting. In one tank, everybody was wounded except one man, Huom, a Kit Carson scout (a former VC or NVA soldier who volunteered to scout for the Americans). He just jumped up to the top of the tank and began firing that .50-caliber until he too got wounded." So intense was the fighting that the cavalry experienced a high machine gun failure rate caused by individuals firing continuous bursts with the weapons. The resultant extreme heat jammed the guns, welding bolts to the barrels.

With approaching nightfall, the 1/1 Cav broke off contact, withdrew about half a mile, and established defensive positions. Although it had been a day of heavy fighting, the combination of armored protection and heavy suppressive fire from all weapons had kept losses tolerably low. The NVA had

Your motto is attack

MOBILITY PLUS FIREPOWER: Cavalry troopers shield their ears from the blast of a 4.2-inch mortar mounted on a circular base plate in the hull of their M-113. When enemy positions were inaccessible to direct-fire, line-of-sight weapons, mortar carriers provided mobile indirect fire support that could strike at enemy positions nearly five miles away.

delivered heavy volumes of fire, but apparently had spent more time ducking the return fire than aiming. US losses included two cavalrymen killed and 23 wounded. Still, this figure meant that about one out of every nine Americans had been hit. Unknown to the 1/1 Cavalry, they had taken on the better part of two NVA regiments.

The second day's plan called for all three cavalry troops, along with two reinforcing infantry companies, to attack the NVA position from various directions. The troopers told to exert frontal pressure found the second day to be a repeat of the first. Whenever they tried to advance on the enemy-held woodline, a blistering wall of fire confronted them.

Nearby, Troop C also experienced trouble.

Brig. Gen. William DePuy —became a convert to armor. As operations officer to Gen. Westmoreland he doubted the effectiveness of armor in Vietnam. Experience taught him otherwise. Later, as commander of the 1st Division, he constantly deployed armored units to seek out the enemy.

Supporting infantry got too far in front of the troop's armor. As Troop C advanced to within 20 yards of the treeline, the defenders opened fire, pinning the supporting infantry to the ground. It prevented the cavalry from returning fire for fear of hitting its own infantry. It was a bad mistake. Eventually, repeated short advances by the tracks and tanks extricated the infantry. But the troop was driven back from the treeline and forced to call in helicopters to evacuate the wounded.

One unit, Troop A, found a gap in the enemy trench-line created by close support aircraft. Thrusting into the woodline, the troop became surrounded by confused NVA soldiers. A chaotic battle resulted without regard to front, flank or rear with both sides

A recovery vehicle is gingerly guided across a riverbed. Negotiating South Vietnam's numerous streams and drainage ditches was always hazardous. Antitank mines and grenades detonated by trip wires were favorite boobytraps of the VC.

continually bumping into one another. Tanks depressed their barrels to fire at the unbelievably close range of 25 yards. In such circumstances tactics played little part. It was a soldier's fight.

Tactics did matter in Troop B's flank attack on the second day. The troop was assigned a blocking position to prevent the foe from retreating. Approaching the fight from a completely new direction deep on the flank of the NVA treeline, the troop quickly encountered heavy resistance. The deadly brew of recoilless rifles, RPGS, and automatic weapons halted the advance. Leaving a platoon to deal with this force, the rest of Troop B bypassed the position and quickly penetrated deep behind the NVA position, landing squarely in the middle of a NVA regimental headquarters. Forming yet another 360-degree perimeter, Troop B's fire ripped through the enemy's rear. Troop B's tracks tore apart the communication wires that linked this headquarters with the front-line fighters in the treeline.

Overnight the American officers laid their plans not knowing that the disruption caused by Troop B had turned the tide. Under cover of nightfall the NVA withdrew all along the front.

The next day, August 26, the 1/1 Cavalry assault attempted to take the entire treeline position from the flank, only to discover the enemy had already fled. Having conceded a considerable head start, the cavalry raced in pursuit of the retreating NVA. The battered enemy regiments were making for the security of mountains less than 10 miles to the northwest. Here they knew the Americans could not follow onto the near-vertical slopes. Even though it was a race between men on machines and men on foot, the cavalrymen could not catch up with the fleeing enemy main force.

The pursuit continued to the base of the mountains on day four. Effective air support, particularly from the unit's air cavalry troop, the Blue Ghosts, kept the enemy on the run. Rocket-firing Cobra gunships hit hostile targets as close as 25 yards in front of the cavalry's lead tanks.

Toward dusk, the enemy soldiers turned to savage the pursuing Americans. A mine detonated beneath an ACAV while it crossed a stream, killing one trooper while wounding four others. So much blown-up metal from the ACAV littered the stream that

mine sweeping operations proceeded extremely slowly. The mine detectors buzzed ominously whenever they encountered the ACAV fragments. The operators couldn't tell if they were finding mines or wreckage.

This bought the NVA valuable time to prepare a bigger strike. Once the cavalry had completed mine sweeping operations, they entered a valley at the base of the mountains. Intense fire poured from the surrounding ridge-line, battering the armored vehicles. An RPG struck the lead tank's turret ring, penetrating its armor and igniting the tank's ammunition. The resulting explosion destroyed the vehicle. As a flame track maneuvered to help, it too was struck and disabled.

More valuable time was spent organizing medical evacuation for the wounded. By the time the cavalry

DUST-OFF:
A troop of ACAVs pulls back from the treeline and lays a flare to summon a dust-off helo to take out their wounded. Fast evacuation of the injured from the battle zone was a significant factor in saving US lives.

assault force went in, the sun had set. The US
forces withdrew to a defensive perimeter for the
night while the NVA retreated into the impenetrable mountains.

During the four-day action, the American cavalry
and their infantry supports lost ten killed and 81
wounded. In addition, one brave Kit Carson scout
had been killed. Later, an intercepted radio message
indicated that the NVA had suffered frightful
casualties in this battle. Fewer than ten armored
vehicles had been lost. The destroyed tank was the
only one lost by the cavalry over six months
combat.

At the battle of Tam Ky one reinforced US cavalry
squadron with about 600 men had bested two
regiments of NVA regulars who fought from fortified
positions. Most of the cavalry had fought aboard
their vehicles. It had taken all their considerable

Your motto is attack

A Bell Huey operates in support of 1/1 ACAVs during operations in I Corps. The innovative combination of helicopters and ACAVs in combat actions was an important development in the way US forces waged the war. Commanders were able to guide operations from helicopters high above the battlefield. Below them recon helos were used to search for the enemy. Once found, support helos were capable of strafing enemy positions only 25 yards ahead of their own ground troops.

firepower to equalize the numerical disparity. The squadron had not held anything back.

For this action and two other subsequent combats, the 1/1 Cavalry received a Valorous Unit Citation. In addition, two troopers were awarded posthumous Distinguished Service Crosses and some 17 cavalry- and infantrymen received Silver Stars.

The armored cavalry's combination of mobility and firepower was its key asset to the US high command. When generals and their staff made time and distance calculations, they often found that armored units could make the quickest transfer to a new front and still arrive with enough firepower to get the job done. Helicopters could transfer men faster, but the canister-firing 90mm tank guns and three machine guns of the ACAV gave the cavalry a punch that the more lightly equipped air-mobile troops lacked.

Clash of Steel

9

**Tank
vs.
tank**

IN EARLY 1969, General Creighton Abrams implemented a major decision that changed the way America pursued the war. Instead of emphasizing large-scale operations designed to bring powerful NVA units to battle, a program of Vietnamization would be vigorously followed. Political changes in Washington most heavily influenced this decision, as the government of Richard Nixon promoted Vietnamization as a policy of rapid buildup of the South Vietnamese military so that US forces could be withdrawn.

Knowledge that the United States was no longer fighting to win made combat life even more difficult for the men serving in Vietnam. Soldiers became increasingly fixated on escaping from Vietnam unscathed on their DEROS (date expected for return from overseas). It was an attitude newcomers often found shocking.

Although overall strategy was based on Vietnamization, most units continued to engage in combat operations. On March 3, 1969, near the Special Forces camp of Ben Het, Sergeants Hugh Havermale and Jerry Jones strained their ears to listen above the din of a mortar bombardment. A thick fog dampened all sounds. However, between the noise of exploding shells, they heard the unmistakable clanking of mechanical treads and the roar of heavy engines. These were sounds that only one other group of Americans had heard since the war began: the sounds of enemy tanks advancing.

About a year earlier, American Green Berets had faced NVA tanks while defending the Lang Vei Special Forces Camp near Khe Sanh. Soviet-built PT-76 amphibious tanks had spearheaded a nocturnal assault against the camp. Unwieldy recoilless

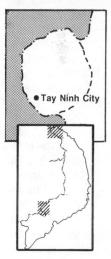

A US infantryman prepares to fire a rocket-propelled grenade against an enemy target. The shaped charge high explosive antitank (HEAT) rockets were effective up to 1,200 yards and could penetrate armor up to four inches. These recoilless rifles were used principally as antibunker weapons.

rifles managed to hold the enemy armor at bay for a while. Then the tanks, accompanied by waves of shock infantry, penetrated the defensive perimeter. Special Forces troops chased them around the camp, trying to hit them with the hand-held Light Antitank Weapons (LAW). Here, as had happened on every battlefield including World War II, the American infantry weapons proved woefully inadequate at stopping armor. Even direct hits glanced off the armor plating. The deadly hunt continued until dawn, with enemy tanks rolling over the defensive positions literally to crush the last resistance. When the US Marines failed to appear from nearby Khe Sanh to rescue the Lang Vei defenders, the final collapse of the base occurred.

Lang Vei had been the first time the North Vietnamese employed armor in South Vietnam and marked the final transition from guerrilla tactics to a conventional struggle between two armies. A year later, for the second encounter with enemy armor, the US forces were much better off than the defenders of Lang Vei. They had tanks of their own.

Sergeants Havermale and Jones belonged to a tank platoon of the 1st Battalion, 69th Armor. Hearing sounds of enemy tanks, they loaded their 90mm tank guns with special high-explosive antitank heat ammunition. Peering intently into the distant gloom, they waited. Sergeant Havermale trained his infrared searchlight into the fog, but he could see nothing.

Then from a little over half a mile away, an explosion ripped the air. An enemy tank had hit an antitank mine. While the PT-76 couldn't move, it could still shoot. Its first round fell short. But it was soon followed by fire from at least seven other enemy tanks. Amid this bombardment, Specialist 4 Frank Hembree was the first tank gunner to return fire: "I only had his muzzle flashes to sight on, but I couldn't wait for a better target because his shells were landing real close to us." Hembree's second shot turned an enemy tank into a fireball.

The American tank commander, Captain John Stovall, radioed to base to request flares from the camp mortars. While these illuminated the NVA tanks, they also showed the enemy where the Americans lay. As Stovall climbed aboard Havermale's tank, an enemy round detonated on the

tank's front armor. The concussion blew Stovall and Havermale free of the tank while killing the driver and loader. The tank itself suffered only slight damage.

Sergeant Jones immediately took charge of the situation . He dismounted from his own tank to run across fireswept ground to another M-48. Jones then directed this tank to a new position where Specialist 4 Eddie Davis sighted the enemy armor. He carefully aimed at the flashes from the enemy muzzles. "I wasn't sure of the target, but I was glad to see it explode a second later."

During the fight, the American tankers expended enormous amounts of ammunition. When they ran out of their basic load of antitank ammo, they had to use normal high-explosive rounds with special fuses. This improvised antitank ammunition failed to inflict damage.

At dawn, a battlefield search turned up two knocked-out PT-76s and one enemy troop carrier. Intelligence later determined that the NVA had planned to use their tanks to overrun the Ben Het base

ENEMY ARMOR: A Russian-built PT-76 light amphibious tank repaired and returned to action after its capture by ARVN forces in Laos. The VC and NVA seldom risked their scarce supply of tanks inside the borders of South Vietnam. This PT-76 is equipped with a 76mm gun and two machine guns.

and destroy the artillery stationed there. Although outnumbered seven to five, American armor foiled them.

When a new set of commanders joined the Blackhorse Regiment, they took a hard look at how armor had been used so far in the war. Their main conclusion was that armor had been excessively roadbound. Too often armor had been given the responsibility of keeping roads open. While this was important, maintaining one's line of communications alone never won any war. Victory required engaging the enemy.

Drawing upon their cavalry heritage, they recalled that the great Indian fighter, General Miles, had concluded that escorting wagon trains and forming

Clash
of steel

JUNGLE BUSTING:
M-48 Patton tanks from 69th Armor crush a path through the underbrush during a search-and-destroy operation. One 52-ton Patton could effectively clear enough room for a column of infantry. But contact between tanks and enemy foot soldiers was rare and was mainly initiated by the enemy

defensive perimeters had been a necessary tactic when faced with surprise attacks. Yet the real way to prevent such attacks was to hit the Indians' camps. Applying this lesson to Vietnam, they resolved to strike out into the jungle. Many skeptics doubted it could be done. Armor officers had observed that foot soldiers slogging through dense, trackless forest had to struggle to advance one half mile per day. Mounted troops could do considerably better. Instead of machete-wielding infantry, a 52-ton Patton tank with a dozer blade welded across the front could lead a jungle penetration column. Such a vehicle could crush all but the largest trees. In addition to providing a path for advancing troops, even in dense jungle a Patton could create an emergency helicopter landing zone in about 15 minutes.

From such thinking the concept of armored "jungle busting" was born. A typical operation occurred in 1969 involving the 1/5 Infantry (Mechanized) of the Tropic Lightning Division. Dismounted infantry plodded through thick underbrush with the platoon leaders walking back and forth just behind to keep the line in order. For over an hour nothing happened. It was later learned that a VC company kept setting ambushes just ahead, waiting for some isolated group to wander too far in advance. When the Americans kept well-ordered lines, the VC had to keep falling back.

Backed up to the edge of a woodlot and afraid to venture into the open, the VC finally attacked. A burst of automatic weapons fire and the whoosh of an RPG began the fight. The rocket penetrated an APC, immobilizing it. All enemy fire was concentrated in front of one platoon of about 20 Americans. The platoon maneuvered to rescue the driver and gunner, when suddenly the welcome roar of an engine announced the arrival of help. Pushing through the underbrush, a big Patton tank came to a halt next to the prone infantry. With his helmeted

RPG HAUL: A cache of enemy weapons captured by 1/5 Infantry. The RPGs with their firing tubes were a feared part of the enemy's arsenal, inflicting almost as much damage as mines. Of limited accuracy, the RPG had a blast that could knock its user over.

head protruding from the turret, a tank commander calmly scanned the ground.

As a track hooked up a cable to drag the damaged M-113 clear, Lieutenant Bill Cooley, a self-confessed "firepower guy," ran to the tank and clambered aboard. Cooley tapped the tank commander on the shoulder and pointed in the direction the RPG round had come from. Speaking through his throat microphone, the tank commander directed the turret to rotate toward the target. The big gun depressed, pointing directly at the presumed target, fired with a roar, reloaded, and fired again. Alternating high explosive and flechette rounds shattered the jungle screen, shredding bark, leaves, and any hidden RPG gunners.

The advance resumed, eventually pushing the VC company out into the open with their backs against a river. Air strikes and artillery finished the job, virtually annihilating the entire enemy force.

Some armor officers wanted to pursue this type of operation deeper into the jungle. However, once tanks entered dense jungle new problems arose. The crews could barely see past their gun barrels through the vines and trailers and elephant grass. Compasses were of little value since as soon as the tanks turned on their electricity, the needles rotated madly. It became the job of the scout helicopters flying overhead to guide the armor on the ground. In triple-canopy jungle this proved difficult.

THE ABILITY of armor to successfully operate off the road surprised almost everyone, friend and foe alike. Before, few commanders had known what to do with armor, particularly during the wet season. Now, the American high command began to better appreciate armor's potential to engage the enemy's main forces. By operating against the VC/NVA's heretofore secure base areas, armor put the enemy light infantry in the difficult bind of either abandoning their bases or trying to defend them against overwhelming firepower.

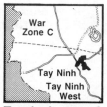

Tactical area of operations for Montana Raider.

The NVA tried both approaches during Operation Montana Raider.

It was to be the first major operation led by the 11th Armored Cavalry's new commander, Lieutenant Colonel James Leach. In a war where all too often the enemy chose the time and place to fight,

Clash of steel

IMPROVED PROTECTION: An M-113 ACAV speeds through a rubber plantation close to Tay Ninh City. The addition of lightweight hollow steel planking suspended over the vehicle sides offered additional protection against the shaped charges fired from enemy RPGs.

Leach had worked hard to achieve surprise in this operation.

The deception plan had involved aerial reconnaissance of an area northwest of Tay Ninh City. During these flights, map overlays marking troop movements and objectives in this area had been deliberately "lost." To heighten the enemy's suspicion, intentional breaches in radio transmissions indicated a buildup preceding a drive into this area. Finally, on April 12, 1969, mechanized elements had driven past the actual area of operations and toward the false target. On April 13, they would change

direction and strike to the northeast of the city in
the hopes that the enemy would be surprised.

The operation was code named "Montana Raider"
in honor of the outgoing commander of the 1st
Cavalry Division, Major General George Forsythe,
who hailed from that western state.

At dawn, Leach was airborne in his command
Huey. A cavalryman to the core, Leach named his
chopper "Traveller," after the famous gray horse
Lee rode during the Civil War. As the helicopter rose
into the air a violent B-52 attack was going in on
the horizon. As the smoke and dust cleared, the

Maj. Gen George Forsythe —outgoing commander of 1st Cavalry Division (Airmobile). Operation Montana Raider was named in honor of his home state.

Blackhorse went in. To get in position they had made a 78-mile route march in eight hours. Now, two squadrons proceeded on a narrow front to limit risk from random mines. The first vehicles cleared a safe path for those that followed. At the front of each "jungle busting" column went the big M-48 tanks, bulldozing a path through the dense vegetation. Behind followed the ACAV, the personnel carrier tracks. The men knew they were supposed to ride inside these vehicles. But here, as throughout Vietnam, they proved resistant to the general's ideas about how the tracks should be employed.

So they rode on the decks, unless their colonel was close by, to escape the heat and to better survive a mine. They could be as vigilant on the back deck as inside, could see more, and could be much more comfortable. Overhead, their commander worried for their safety, knowing that an RPG round might hit only one crew member if they stayed inside. Such a round exploding on the outside of the deck could wipe out the entire crew. On into the mission area drove the Blackhorse, dodging craters caused by the aerial bombardment.

Just above the trees, the rotor blades of the tiny OH-6A "Loach" scout helicopters fanned the treetops. The pilots, usually operating in teams of two, kept in constant communication with the armor. About 1,000 feet above them flew the lethal Cobra gunships, combining tremendous firepower with the ability to deliver it with pinpoint accuracy in a matter of seconds. Stacked over the gunships were the squadron commander's helicopters. Rather than ride in the armored fighting vehicles where their vision would be badly restricted by the terrain, they stayed overhead where they could better direct their vehicles. This was at some cost in casualties as command choppers were often the target of intense enemy fire. At least one mechanized unit commander took some basic lessons in flying helicopters so that he had some hope of crash-landing safely if his pilot was hit.

Finally, on top of it all flew "Traveller," with the regiment commander aboard. Warfare had passed through many technical evolutions as communications developed. A commander's ability to direct a battle increased tremendously from the time of the Civil War, when a general's knowledge was limited by what he could see with the sweep of a telescope or what he was told by messengers riding upon hard-charging horses, to World War Two, when a commander tried to piece together radio reports in order to adjust the tactical map and comprehend what the men on the ground were facing. In Vietnam, the commander hovered right overhead. Consequently, he had an unprecedented opportunity to "micromanage," to issue orders directly to small units and skip links in the chain of command.

Many commanders operated this way. Leach's predecessor as the Blackhorse commander, Colonel George Patton, had been renowned for his front-line leadership, swooping down in his helicopter (named Little Sorrel after Stonewall Jacksons's horse) to land amidst the front-line troops and influence events personally. Wounded in World War II while serving in a tank force, Leach well knew what the men on the ground confronted. He conceived the commander's role differently. He believed his job was to offer help when needed, arrange for air strikes or artillery support, and let his subordinates fight the battle. Now, in a new war, he was putting his concept of armored command to its first test.

First contact came when some dismounted cavalrymen assessing B-52 bomb damage received fire. The armored units rushed to assist them. While

THE RIGHT WAY: Rare view of troops of 1st Cav (Airmobile) riding inside their ACAV. Most preferred to disregard orders and ride on top to get as far away as possible from any potential mine blast. Riding inside astride sandbags and empty ammo boxes was an acceptable compromise that also provided protection against RPG attacks.

some vehicles halted to engage the enemy frontally, others branched off the main column to encircle the enemy on both flanks.

Then the tanks and tracks beat down a cleared space around the enemy position. To escape, the VC/NVA would have to cross this zone through a hail of automatic fire from the vehicles and a fusillade of rockets from patrolling helicopters. Next, the cavalry vehicles increased the pressure by crisscrossing through the enemy position, firing at any target thus revealed. From the shelter of their APCs, the mechanized infantry blasted away at close range

Clash of steel

AERIAL RETRIEVAL: A sling is hooked around an M-113 up to its tracks in the mud of a rice paddy. The bogged down M-113's 19,000-lb payload was well within the lifting capacity of this Ch-47 "Chinook" helicopter from 242d Battalion, a medium helicopter outfit that sported a kicking mule emblem and answered to the call sign "Muleskinners."

with grenade launchers. The heavy contacts vindicated Leach's deception operations. The enemy, expecting the Blackhorse elsewhere, fought at a disadvantage.

For most of a week, the 11th Armored Cavalry maintained the initiative, sweeping through sanctuary areas (until then thought safe by the enemy). The NVA had long used this area as a rear service and transportation zone for men entering South Vietnam from Cambodia. Having never faced armor before, they tended to stay and defend their base camps. It was a mistake not made by their comrades with more battle experience. The regiment withdrew to a secure base camp for two days of badly needed maintenance. Then, in Phase II of Montana Raider, it sortied out to attack the same area from a different direction. Here, along the border of War Zone C, the Blackhorse again demonstrated skillful use of fire and maneuver tactics. Operating in dense jungle, the regiment demonstrated that armored units could cross difficult terrain to strike at the enemy. The great value of these strikes was in the firepower of the tanks. When enemy troops were found they were usually well dug-in. A unit inserted by helicopter would have to winkle such an enemy out with hand grenades and flamethrowers. A mechanized unit could rely upon the tank cannon in the assault.

The Blackhorse turned around again to enter an area of rubber plantations along the Saigon River. This Phase III proved the least productive portion of Montana Raider. Monotonous ground searches uncovered small caches of rice and ammunition, but overall the enemy avoided contact. When the operation ended, 45 Blackhorse troopers had been killed and 240 wounded. The VC/NVA suffered some 250 killed. Twenty tanks had been hit, eight of which were wrecks. Three ACAVs had been knocked out and another ten damaged. Clearly, tanks had been the spearhead into combat.

When Montana Raider finished, some tanks had traveled over 1,000 miles according to their odometer readings. Even more remarkable, 800 miles were across difficult jungle terrain that was without a modern road network. The engineers had to use their armored-vehicle-launched bridges no less than 17 times to keep the column rolling over streams and ravines.

General Forsythe, for whom the operation was named, rightly observed that the 1,000-mile jungle penetration was a grand movement worthy of some of the great armored sweeps in World War II. It was also a modern lesson in armored tactics emphasizing mobility and firepower. The US forces also learned about the limits of armor in the jungle. They found that while tracked vehicles could be used in almost any terrain, there was a high penalty in wear and tear on the vehicles. For every ten days spent jungle busting, five would then have to be used for

A tank crew member trying to lever loose a jammed track on an M-48. Tanks paid a high price in wear and tear during jungle busting operations.

HEAVY ROLLER: With mines responsible for over 50 percent of armor losses, field commanders requested devices better able to deal with this constant threat. The inventors' solution was this road-only mineroller that in theory could detect and detonate low-density mines. Individual rollers were replaceable, though this was a lengthy process. Tank crews disliked the device, claiming that the 20-ton weight made suspension front-heavy and steering difficult. But when tested on a combat engineers' vehicle, the rollers detonated four mines and the engineers requested more.

maintenance and rest. Debris would have to be removed from crew compartments, filters changed, radiators drained, and engines overhauled.

The extremely rough ride during a jungle busting operation jarred loose much of the delicate mechanical equipment inside a tank. One squadron leader found that the crucial linkages that allowed aimed fire from the main tank gun had become so out of line that the crews were reduced to merely pointing in the general direction of the enemy and blasting away.

Into the Sanctuary

10

The invasion of Cambodia

HOWEVER Vietnamization might appear to the Pentagon, it proved difficult to implement in the field. Except for a few elite ARVN units, for years the bulk of the hard fighting had been conducted by American units. Now ARVN units who had been engaged in rear area pacification programs suddenly were required to operate in the front line against hardened enemy regulars. The result proved very mixed.

A machinegunner in the 1/1 Cav recalls that suddenly his unit was operating in tandem with under-motivated ARVN soldiers. Where previously the Americans had formed a cohesive four-man team on each ACAV, now up to 14 ARVN soldiers tended to get in the way. On the interior bed of the vehicle, the ACAV troopers kept can after can of machine gun ammunition at the ready. In a firefight, their automatic weapons rapidly used it up. Clear access to this ammo sometimes meant the difference between life and death.

With the Vietnamese aboard, the gunners had to work around the extra bodies to reload their weapons. Worse, all too often when the enemy opened fire, the ARVN soldiers dived down the hatches to hide behind the armor plating. US cavalrymen remember physically tossing them overboard in their frantic attempts to get at the ammunition.

With patience and training, improvements could be made. Increasing numbers of armored soldiers devoted themselves to ARVN training. But the accelerating pace of US troop withdrawals left little time. A wide array of training techniques were tried, ranging from sophisticated exercises on gunnery courses supervised by experienced American NCOs, to simple motivational bulletins and placards. One 11th Armored Cavalry colonel handed out cards

Into the sanctuary

MINE DETECTION:
Casualties from mines continued to grow alarmingly in the late '60s and early '70s. Many mines were rust- and mud-encrusted relics as this Marine officer (left) is discovering. Discarded US mess tins and ammo boxes were often used by the VC to make mines and booby traps. The most effective detection method was to prod the ground gently with a hand-held probe like the spear-like pole used by this engineer (right).

to all ARVN officers he met. They read in English and Vietnamese, "An organization does well only those things the boss checks." But it was impossible to instill a leadership tradition using placards and pep talks.

FOR THE American units that continued combat operations, mines and booby traps remained the most feared enemy. In 1970 most new soldiers in the 1/1 Cav were dumped with the disagreeable task of driving the armored personnel carriers. Seated next

to the engine, the driver's position was hot and un-
comfortable. His body was vulnerable to any mines
that the track might detonate, his head—which pro-
truded outside the armor protection—was exposed
to small arms and shell fire.

New drivers had to concentrate hard on the task
of driving. They tried to follow exactly in the wake
of the vehicle in front, the idea being that a
preceding vehicle would detonate any explosives.
New drivers were warned about the rookie mistake
of becoming confused and driving in old vehicle

tracks. These old tracks were the favorite site for enemy mines. But death could come suddenly even to those who steered perfectly, and it was usually the drivers who paid the price.

Simultaneous with Vietnamization came a significant decline in the morale of the American combat soldier. As General Westmoreland wrote: "It was only after the start of American withdrawal in 1969 that serious morale and disciplinary problems arose." No one bothered to tell the front-line soldier why he faced the continuing dangers of combat while some men went home. The unfair draft system, which drew most soldiers from lower income groups, caused resentment among active-duty soldiers. The disproportionate number of ethnic minority members increased racial tensions. The growing antiwar movement in the United States filled soldiers with doubt about their mission. Groups tended to polarize: country versus city, blacks versus whites, "Yankees" against "rebels," Californians against New Yorkers. Drug abuse increased.

Gen. William Westmoreland — with the US withdrawal came problems of morale.

For most men any thoughts of winning the war had faded. Rather they focused on surviving their tour. Many of the small unit commanders shared this mind set. As the war dragged on, these commanders concentrated on getting their men back safely rather then hurting the enemy.

The men serving after 1968 were a considerable change from the spit-and-polish soldiers of the early days in Vietnam. An executive officer in the 1/1 Cav wrote about this new breed of soldier: "He likes women, beer, ice cream, Playboy magazine, letters from 'The World,' Australia, steaks, 'DEROS,' hot showers, Hong Kong, and hot chow. He isn't much for the monsoons, RPGs, AK-47s, spit and polish, broken torsion bars, C-rations, roast beef, Kool Aid, powdered eggs, 'Charlie,' walking, or waiting in line. No one else is so early in the chow line, or so often at the beer cooler. When you want him he's somewhere in the AO (area of operations). When you don't want him he's hovering over your desk with 117 reasons why he should be promoted or go on a third R&R." Such tolerance for behavior that would formerly have been considered out of bounds came about because regular Army officers recognized the stresses of waging an unpopular war with citizen soldiers.

The invasion of Cambodia gave many armored units new purpose. This was an operation soldiers could understand. For years the VC/NVA had used the artificial sanctuary of Cambodia to prepare attacks against targets in Vietnam. Now the Americans could hit back. Although it was a different looking soldier who took part in these operations, they advanced with élan seldom seen since the first units came to Vietnam. with M-60 machine guns hanging at hip-level, jungle fatigue shirts open to expose peace beads or religious chains dangling across dust-caked chests, while over their long hair, tolerated as a front-line privilege, they wore cut-down bush hats.

THE CAMBODIAN invasion was a massive "spoiling attack" designed to seriously hamper the NVA buildup and buy time for Vietnamization to take hold. At dawn on May 1, 1970, the heavy artillery fell silent as the last B-52s finished their bombing runs. A roar of engines replaced the sound of explosions as APCs and tanks began Operation Toan Thang (Total Victory) 43. Among the objectives was the elusive enemy headquarters (COSVN) for

HOME COMFORTS: A Red Cross 'Doughnut Dollie' delivers mail and chats with troopers in their ACAV. Older hands complained that post-1968 draftees showed too little enthusiasm for combat and too much for creature comforts.

military operations in South Vietnam. While many previous operations had futilely sought after COSVN, by now American intelligence had rather precisely located it. Situated on the Mimot rubber plantation about seven miles into Cambodia, this headquarters lay squarely in the path of one prong of the planned allied invasion. In addition, the generals hoped that major NVA units would be brought to open battle. The impressive armored firepower of the 11th Armored Cavalry; 2d Battalion, 34th Armor; and 2d Battalion, 47th

Into the sanctuary

Company A, 2d Squadron, 1st Cav line up their ACAVs as they prepare to move out for the Cambodian border in May 1970. Behind the first armored personnel carrier are four high-sided M-557s, variants of the M-113s that served as command posts. The basic M-113 superstructure was built up into a fully enclosed box that in the 100° heat of Vietnam required its own air conditioning.

Infantry, would be available should the enemy stand and fight. In addition, the 1st ARVN Armored Cavalry and various American and Vietnamese dismounted troops joined the attack.

The 11th Armored Cavalry formed the northernmost prong of the invasion. In order for the regiment to assemble, the 3d Squadron had moved over 180 miles in two days just before the attack. As the preparatory bombardment lifted, ACAVs and Sheridan reconnaissance tanks fanned out to lead the way, followed by heavier Patton tanks. A small

A captured NVA soldier is escorted to a helicopter to be flown back to base for interrogation. Although the excursion into Cambodia failed to enagage the enemy in large-scale combat it provided US intelligence with a rich supply of information about the enemy's intentions and organization.

stream bordered by several hundred yards of swamp marked the border. Here several tanks bogged down and had to be towed clear.

In the late afternoon of May 1, scout helicopters radioed to lead elements of the 2d Squadron that an enemy force lay dug in on the far side of a clearing some four miles inside Cambodia. Almost before the unit could react, hostile fire erupted from three sides.

A combined helicopter/armor assault cleared out the NVA position. The 2d Squadron struck the enemy's flank while helicopters patrolled likely avenues of enemy withdrawal. In this fashion some 50 enemy soldiers were killed at a cost of two Americans.

Overall, the hopes for big battles proved vain once again as scout helicopters quickly spotted large groups of fleeing NVA troops. Instead the attackers had to content themselves with seizing and destroying the abundant supplies that were uncovered as the armor penetrated into Cambodia. The size and complexity of the NVA bases staggered the searchers. Vast amounts of ammunition and food were found, often along with the cargo trucks used to bring them down from the north.

The next day, ARVN troops entered the battle in a big way. Over 250 ACAVs from five cavalry regiments lined up abreast at 25-yard intervals on a 3.5-mile front. On signal they swept forward, overwhelming enemy resistance.

On May 3, the Blackhorse received a dream assignment. The regiment was ordered to attack north along Route 7 toward the important road junction of Snuol. The advance lay through large rubber plantations, as good a tank terrain as one could expect in Southeast Asia. After breaking out of the jungle, the lead tanks of the 2d Squadron raced ahead at speeds of up to 40 miles per hour. They stopped only three times at places where bridges had been blown. The armor-vehicle-launched bridge then trundled to the front to lay a new bridge. As soon as engineers secured the far end of the bridge, the cavalry was off again. It proved an exhilarating advance which the troops later referred to as their "Cambodian Blitz." One senior officer said: "This Cambodian operation is pure blitzkrieg, like something from a World War II Panzer Division's book of tactics." Colonel Donn Starry planned to use his armor to encircle the town of Snuol. However, one prong of the pincer movement became entangled in heavy combat while moving through a large rubber plantation on the city's outskirts. An exploding grenade disabled Starry and put an end to the planned encirclement. The colonel's replacement ordered a recon troop of ACAVs and Sheridans to advance into Snuol.

The scouts encountered heavy NVA small arms and machine gun fire. Just short of the central marketplace, the lead Sheridan received an RPG round. The column immediately herringboned—alternate vehicles facing left and right, able to fire to both sides of the road—and returned the fire. Another RPG hit the already damaged Sheridan. Within a minute the second Sheridan was struck as well. For five minutes the scouts fired back with tank machine guns. Under cover of this fire they slowly retreated amid a hail of rifle, RPG, and mortar fire.

Apparently the NVA fight had been a rear-guard action designed to allow the bulk of their troops to escape. When Patton tanks passed through the scouts and advanced to engage the enemy, the NVA put up considerably less resistance. The big tanks' heavy fire blasted the North Vietnamese from the city. Unlike other instances when armor had become bogged down in house-to-house fighting, the Blackhorse's rapid advance and heavy firepower carried the day.

An analysis of the operation determined that armor and aviation had played a vital, aggressive role. Overall, however, many American units had been understandably reluctant to take combat risks. Their emphasis had been on minimizing losses. These units knew very well that they were soon to depart from Vietnam. No one wanted to be the last in his unit to die.

As a test of Vietnamization the operation revealed several important problems. ARVN units relied excessively on American firepower. Many ARVN field officers proved unable to call in this firepower without help from American advisers. Too often ARVN units maneuvered with great timidity. Such difficulties were to become all too apparent in the following year's invasion of Laos.

An M-551 Sheridan tank —fast and light with a top speed of 44 mph, it was ideally suited to the "blitzkrieg" style of the Cambodian invasion.

Assault on Saigon

The Spring Offensive 1972

Perhaps no statistic about armor is more telling than the proportion of armor that remained in Vietnam as American troop withdrawals proceeded. As entire divisions left the country, the American high command had to determine which units to leave behind. The number of troops that remained was a political decision made in Washington. The generals could decide which specific units stayed and they usually chose armor.

Following the attack into Cambodia in 1970, more than 139,000 Americans returned home. But most armor remained. By the end of 1970, the concentration of armor in the remaining combat units rose to 46 percent. One year later, following the transfer of another 158,000 soldiers home, this figure rose to 54 percent.

The Vietnamization program continued through 1971. In that year headquarters decided upon one last, major joint offensive to take advantage of remaining American units. The drive into Cambodia had significantly slowed enemy operations along the border; perhaps a similar attack into the Laotian panhandle could achieve the same results.

The attack was to be spearheaded by South Vietnamese troops, aided by American air and artillery power. The kick-off came with an all-American operation, Dewey Canyon II, designed to open up Route 9 so ARVN units could drive into Laos.

Before dawn on January 30, 1971, a tank dozer belonging to the 1st Brigade, 5th Infantry Division headed along Route 9 toward the now abandoned Marine base at Khe Sahn. Following the dozer came 1st Brigade reinforced with two mechanized, one cavalry, and one tank battalion.

The plan called for the column to push on near the

Laotian border where fire support bases would be established to support the ARVN attack. The big self-propelled, long-range guns of the 108th Artillery Group trundled along with the column to man these bases. With the 1/1 Cav racing ahead, engineers carved a road out of sheer mountain cliffs to allow the guns to roll on. A week later all was ready for the ARVN attack.

Supported by a massive artillery bombardment as well as numerous B-52 strikes, the attack achieved initial success. US air power had a field day knocking out petroleum pipelines that sent giant fireballs billowing up into the clouds. The elaborate NVA base area appeared to be at the allies' mercy.

Then the NVA counterattacked the flanks of the

Assault on Saigon

SNIPER ATTACK: Americal Division troopers from 1/1 Cav take cover from sniper and RPG fire along Route 9, the fiercely contested road corridor into Laos. Piles of shell cases on the ACAV decks and empty ammo boxes testify to the intensity of the firefight. The trooper standing on the right-hand track is trying to lift a wounded gunner to safety as the brush around the ACAVs begins to burn.

ARVN invasion force. Tank-led infantry columns surprised and routed ARVN units. Overhead, American helicopters time and time again stemmed the tide, running out of ammunition before they could destroy all the NVA armor. Under heavy enemy pressure the South Vietnamese forces' hurried retreat turned into an ugly rout. A roadbound ARVN armored convoy became caught in a massive ambush. Men abandoned their vehicles as American gunships had to be called in to destroy the ARVN tanks and artillery before NVA forces could capture them.

The invasion of Laos had the code name Lam Son 719. The code name commemorated a famous victory in early Vietnamese history. Lam Son had been

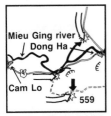

April 1, 1972 — path of the NVA attack along Route 9 south of the DMZ.

chosen in hopes of inspiring ARVN forces to duplicate the efforts of their ancestors. While some individual ARVN units fought gallantly, overall Lam Son 719 turned into a disaster.

By the beginning of 1972 an encouraging lull in combat allowed most US ground forces to leave uneventfully. Troop F, 17th Cavalry left Da Nang on April 6 after conducting the last US ground armored operation in Vietnam. Four days later, the 1st Squadron, 1st Cavalry began to leave, the last such force to depart.

Knowing the dates of the US evacuation, the North Vietnamese high command bided their time. As the Year of the Rat began in February 1972, they prepared to return to their real goal, conquering South Vietnam. Four years earlier they had committed their army to directly challenge American forces during the Tet Offensive. It had taken them this long to recover the physical strength to try again. Only this time the American ground forces were gone. Vietnamization was about to be truly tested.

As US and South Vietnamese intelligence officers evaluated the enemy's options, they dismissed the threat posed by enemy armor. Until then, NVA armor had appeared on only three battlefields. Yet there were disquieting signs for those who looked intently. Scout helicopters of the 4th Cavalry had found numerous tread marks near Krek, Cambodia, where the NVA had apparently staged a practice assault against an abandoned allied base. In addition, intelligence officers could have looked at their own experience, with its many examples of successful armored operations. Instead, they underestimated the North Vietnamese Army.

On paper the South Vietnamese Army had more armor then ever. The pride of the force was the 20th Tank Regiment, the first such ARVN unit in history. American advisers had worked intensively with this unit to make it combat ready. Numerous problems hampered the training. Some 60 percent of the regiment's tanks had serious mechanical problems beyond the capability of the crew to fix. Missing repair and technical manuals, the language barrier, rapid manpower turnover, and related problems kept the 20th from becoming a top-line unit.

To date, ARVN tankers had exclusively used the M-41 light tank. This tank had no range finder. The

20th received the M-48, which depended upon a complex rangefinder and ballistic computer. The mechanism baffled the ARVN soldiers. Their language didn't even have a word for ballistic computer; it got translated as "adding machine." Before they were really ready, the 20th went into battle. At the end of March, the NVA launched all-out assaults from across the DMZ nominally separating North from South Vietnam and from the A Shau valley.

This was no guerrilla war. It was a classically conventional attack, begun by massed artillery and rocket fire and spearheaded by tanks. Frantic messages came to the 20th Regiment to rapidly move to Quang Tri City. The outlying posts between Quang Tri and the DMZ had been overrun or evacuated. Only the Mieu Giang River stood between the NVA and the province capital. The South Vietnamese commander, General Vu Van Giai, ordered the 20th to attack to stabilize the defensive position along this river.

First the regiment attacked west to give help to the embattled ARVN 11th Armored Cavalry Regiment. With 44 tanks, it set off cross-country, overrunning a surprised NVA ambush team.

Having repulsed enemy probes during the night, the 20th learned the next day that large NVA forces,

TARGET DESTROYED: A Russian-built T-54 sits in a rice paddy after being destroyed by ARVN forces as it attempted to move along Route 9. The ARVN tankers, newly equipped with M-48s, exacted a heavy toll against the ill-trained NVA armor.

including tanks, were heading toward the Mieu Giang River bridge at Dong Ha. The regiment hustled into position to block this enemy movement.

About noon, ARVN tankers saw an NVA mechanized column driving south toward Dong Ha. It was a sight that would have made any tanker salivate. At last, the possibility of tank-to-tank dueling, just like US tankers had prepared for in Europe. The ARVN tankers recognized the opportunity as well. Moving into concealed positions, they waited for the NVA to get closer. At a range of nearly 1.5 miles the ARVN Pattons opened fire.

Their opening barrage knocked out nine light PT-76 amphibious tanks as well as two formidable T-54s. The NVA clearly had been caught by surprise.

South Vietnamese headquarters eavesdropping on the NVA radio network heard the enemy commander shout in surprised disbelief at losing his valuable tanks to an enemy he could not see. At this stage NVA armored units committed many mistakes characteristic of armor fighting in their first battle. An American analyst wrote, "Their hesitant, uncoordinated fumbling with some well-maintained Soviet vehicles showed once again that successful armor employment is totally dependent on aggressive spirit and technical skill."

For eight more days "the Rock of Dong Ha" held steady against increasing enemy pressure. On April 9, another tank-to-tank duel occurred. The gunnery training of the ARVN tankers paid impressive

THE END:
April 30, 1975,
11.50 A.M.
The first North Vietnamese tank smashes down the doors of the presidential palace in Saigon. The palace was later renamed the "Palace of Liberation."

North Vietnamese tankers armed with AK-47s stand guard over their crippled T-54 at Tan Son Nhut airport on the outskirts of Saigon. The tank was damaged during fierce fighting that led to the fall of the capital.

dividends as they destroyed 16 T-54s at ranges over 1.5 miles. Badly hurt, the NVA required 15 days to regroup.

Near Dong Ha on April 23, the enemy employed a new weapon, a Soviet-made Sagger wire-guided missile. This weapon allowed the crew to fire the projectile and then steer it toward its target. At first the ARVN tankers remained mesmerized by the missile's slow, erratic flight. A Patton tank and an ACAV blew up. In succeeding days, eight ARVN tanks were hit and completely destroyed. With experience, the 20th Regiment learned appropriate countermeasures.

On April 27, the NVA began a new assault against the ARVN river position. Brutal artillery fire disrupted the defenders. The barrage was followed by skillful, aggressive NVA tank and infantry attacks. By mid-morning all officers in one of the 20th's squadrons had become casualties. The defensive line collapsed as ARVN forces were overrun. During a fighting withdrawal, the 20th's accurate tank fire knocked out another five T-54s. But the unit was down to 18 operational Patton tanks, and by May 2, when the regiment finally managed to break contact every one of its tanks had been lost.

The NVA Spring Offensive of 1972 was eventually halted, but only by the narrowest margin. Only the intervention of American air power had staved off defeat. The American introduction of their own version of a wire-guided missile, the tube-launched, optically-tracked, wire-guided (TOW) missile, had been one example of the impact of American air power. A demonstration team arrived in Saigon on April 24. By May 2 they were out hunting the NVA.

The TOWs were mounted on Huey helicopters. After firing, thin wire extended from the missile back to the operator. This allowed a crewman to send signals to the missile to adjust its flight. By manipulating hand-held controls with the aid of display screens, the operator made in-flight corrections until the missile hit the target. The whole arrangement was not too dissimilar from the arcade video games that would soon delight the public back in the States. In real combat, TOW-armed Hueys became flying, highly accurate antitank weapons.

Further success came in support of the ARVN 23d Infantry Division. This division had trained hard in antitank tactics. Interestingly, it was led by Colonel Ly Tong Ba, the same officer who in 1963 had disregarded his American adviser's advice and successfully led a mounted charge against a VC position in the delta. Continuing his armor career, Ba now led his men in a neat defense of Highway 14 against an NVA tank/infantry attack. His antitank gunners battered the attackers, leaving American air power to pick off the remnants. Two heavy T-54 tanks fell to the TOW team.

May 26 proved the climactic day for the TOW teams. Flying above Kontum City, a TOW team of Chief Warrant Officers Edmund Smith and Danny Rowe destroyed six enemy tanks moving through the city streets. A second TOW team knocked off another three. During its first combat employment, the TOW had shown itself to be an extremely accurate, deadly weapon. Within their initial month of use, TOWs registered 47 confirmed kills, including 24 tanks.

When reviewing successes and failures, the NVA high command had to consider the impact of TOWs as well as the rest of the American aerial arsenal. They had learned how decisive this could be during their Tet Offensive in 1968. Now again, in 1972, air power had reigned supreme. The VC/NVA resolved that they would not attack again until they were sure potent American air power was unavailable to prop up the ARVN ground forces.

The Congressional Medal of Honor, the nation's highest award for gallantry, was awarded to 155 soldiers during the Vietnam war. Nineteen of the recipients served in armored units.

NOT UNTIL 1975 were the North Vietnamese sufficiently confident of American intentions to risk another large scale assault. This time NVA generals planned it to be the final attack. Armor would play a vital role in their plan. NVA armor had realized significant improvements in both training and equipment. In 1972, rocket-armed South Vietnamese infantry had knocked out numerous tanks at close range. In response, NVA tanks were fitted with light side "spaced-armor" to create an extra skin to explode the charge before it penetrated the main armor. It was the same technique used on American M-113s to resist rocket grenades.

The NVA also improved their command and control of tanks. Before, armor would mill about in confusion when engaged unexpectedly. By 1975, superior communications and training gave them

Assault on Saigon

BORN IN AN M-113: The war is coming to an end, but for this baby life has just begun in an M-113. Transformed by her Viet Cong father into an improvised maternity ward with bales of hay, the APC was to serve as the family home for the months ahead while the reconstruction of their home near Cu Chi took place. For the M-113, the most versatile armored vehicle employed by the US forces, this was one peaceful use its creators had not foreseen.

the ability to react more quickly to a changing battlefield situation.

The all-out NVA assault began in late 1974. By the first months of 1975 it had taken on aspects of the Nazi tank blitz of France in 1940. In 1940, terror stricken civilians had jammed vital roads preventing reserves from meeting the attack. The same thing happened in South Vietnam. General Le Nguyen Khang reported that in the northern provinces over 1.5 million refugees clogged the roads. "The chaos and disorder were indescribable. Hunger, looting, and crimes were widespread. Traffic was impossible. To maneuver, tanks had to make

headway by crushing people first." The situation steadily worsened as tank panic gripped the nation.

While some steady units continued to fight hard, in many places the mere appearance of an NVA tank caused the defenders to flee in panic. Soon several tank-led columns closed upon Saigon itself.

At 10 A.M. on April 30, 1975, as flag bedecked NVA armored fighting vehicles rolled into Saigon's streets, President Ho Chi Minh ordered the South Vietnamese armed forces to cease fighting.

A "guerrilla" war had ended most conventionally with one side's tanks capturing the opponent's capital.

ACAV	— Armored cavalry assault vehicle.
AK-47	— Russian-designed 'Kalishnikov' gas-operated 7.62mm automatic rifle with effective range of 400m.
APC	— Armored personnel carrier.
ARP	— Aerorifle platoon.
Arty	— Artillery.
ARVN	— Army of the Republic of Vietnam (S. Vietnam).
AT	— Antitank.
ATGW	— Antitank guided weapon.
Bde	— Brigade.
Beehive	— Artillery rounds filled with thousands of small metal fléchettes which burst in a 30° arc.
BLT	— Battalion landing team.
Bn	— Battalion.
CINCPAC	— Commander in Chief, Pacific
Claymore	— A command-detonated antipersonnel land mine which explodes in a 60° fan-shaped swathe.
CTZ	— Corps Tactical Zone, principal military and political territorial sub-division of the republic of S. Vietnam.
DMZ	— Demilitarized Zone. Established by the 1954 Geneva accords, provisionally dividing N. Vietnam from S. Vietnam along the seventeenth parallel.
FSB	— Fire Support Base.
HEAT	— High explosive, anti-tank.
Iron Triangle	— Area to the northwest of Saigon that was the scene of heavy fighting between US and communist forces.
JCS	— Joint Chiefs of Staff. Consists of the chairman, army chiefs of staff, chief of naval operations, air force chief of staff and marine commandant. It exists to advise the president on military policy.
JGS	— Joint General Staff (S. Vietnam).

Kit Carson Scouts	— Viet Cong defectors, recruited to serve as scouts, interpreters and intelligence agents.
LAW	— M-72 light antitank weapon. A shoulder-fired 66mm rocket with a one-time disposable fiberglass launcher.
LRRP	— Long-range reconaissance patrolling.
LZ	— Landing Zone usually a small clearing secured temporarily for the landing of resupply helicopters.
MACV	— Military Assistance Command, Vietnam. US command for all US military activities in Vietnam.
Napalm	— Incendiary used in Vietnam by French and American forces as both a defoliant and antipersonnel weapon.
NVA	— North Vietnamese Army. Often used colloquially to refer to a soldier of the NVA in the same way that 'ARVN' was used to designate a S. Vietnamese soldier.
Ontos	— Marine weapon consisting of six 106mm recoilless rifles mounted coaxially on a tracked chassis.
RPG	— Rocket-propelled grenade.
Sapper	— VC commando, usually armed with explosives.
Tet	— The lunar New Year, celebrated throughout S. Vietnam.
TOW	— Tube-launched, optically-tracked, wire-guided missile. An American anti-tank-guided missile.
USMC	— United States Marine Corps.
VC	— Viet Cong.
Vietnamization	— Term given to President Nixon's phased withdrawal of US troops and transfer of their responsibilities to South Vietnam.

About the Author

James R. Arnold

James R. Arnold is a freelance writer who has contributed to numerous military journals and is the author of a history of the US Army Corps of Engineers' role in the Lincoln Memorial.

A specialist on the Napoleonic campaigns, he has written on Napoleon's marshals and is writing a study of Napoleon's 1809 campaign. He is also writing a historical novel about the Civil War, centered on the Blue Ridge Mountains near Berryville, Virginia, where he lives.

Born in 1952 in Harvey, Illinois, James R. Arnold spent his formative years overseas and, encouraged by his parents, used the opportunity to study the sites of famous battles. Tours of Normandy and the Ardennes, coupled with a visit to Paris for Napoleon's bicentennial, prompted him to pursue historical study. After graduating from Colby College, he became a freelance writer, and encouraged by scholars at the UK's Sandhurst Military Academy, he had his first work published in the British Journal of the Society for Army Historical Research.

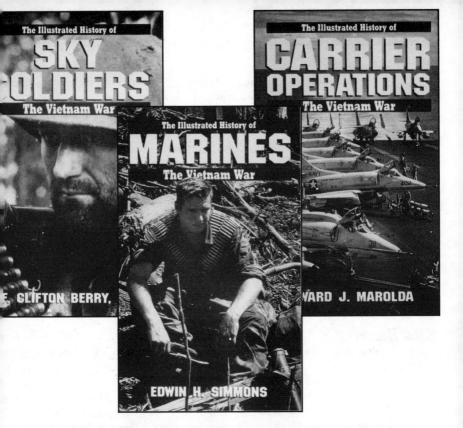

THE ILLUSTRATED HISTORY OF THE VIETNAM WAR

antam's Illustrated History of the Vietnam War is a unique and new series of books exploring in depth the war that seared America to the core: a war that cost 58,022 American lives, that saw great heroism and resourcefulness mixed with terrible destruction and tragedy.

The Illustrated History of the Vietnam War examines exactly what happened: every significant aspect—the physical details, the operations and the strategies behind them—is analyzed in short, crisply written original books by established historians and journalists.

Some books are devoted to key battles and campaigns, others unfold the stories of elite groups and fighting units, while others focus on the role of specific weapons and tactics.

Each volume is totally original and is richly illustrated with photographs, line drawings, and maps.

AVAILABLE NOW

Sky Soldiers
F.Clifton Berry, Jr

The 173d Airborne was the first major American ground combat unit to launc
offensive operations in a major parachute attack. And they were the last out. Thi
is their story. $6.95/$8.95 in Canada ISBN:0-553-34320

Marines
General Edwin H. Simmons

The Marines were the first combat troops into Vietnam and the last to leave. The
bore an even greater proportion of the fighting than in any previous America
war—living up to their legendary fighting tradition in the hard-fought siege of Co
Thien and in the bitter street battle for Hue. $6.95/$8.95 in Canada ISBN:0-553-34448

Carrier Operations
Edward J. Marold

Yankee and Dixie Stations...just two map coordinates in the South China Sea. Bu
for the duration of the Vietnam War they were home to thousands of sailors o
board the aircraft carriers of the US Seventh Fleet. It was from these offshore oase
that US aircraft waged the heaviest bombing campaign in history.
$6.95/$8.95 in Canada ISBN:0-553-34348

OCTOBER 1987

Khe Sanh
Mike Ewin

For 77 days without adequate supplies of water or ammo 6,000 isolated Marine
defended the remote rust-red plateau of Khe Sanh. In the White House an anx
ious president declared that Khe Sanh must not fall. This account tells how clos
the US came to losing one of the most controversial actions of the wa
$6.95/$8.95 in Canada ISBN:0-553-34458

Tunnel Warfare
Tom Mangold & John Penycat

The secret network of tunnels around Saigon was the battleground for the mos
harrowing campaign of the war. This was combat at its most claustrophobic. Arme
with often nothing more than knives, pistols, and flashlights, US volunteers, know
as "Tunnel Rats," took on Viet Cong guerillas, who had lived for years belo
ground. On both sides there were heroes and moments of incredible courag
This account does justice to the men who fought underground.
$6.95/$8.95 in Canada ISBN:0-553-34318

DECEMBER 1987

Artillery
James R. Arnol

Firepower superiority was critical to the US war effort. The solution was a syster
of linked hilltop Fire Support Bases—a unique development in the use of artillery
$6.95/$8.95 in Canada ISBN:0-553-34319

Riverine Force
Victor Croiza

The compelling story of the hastily-assembled brown water navy faced with th
nightmare task of securing South Vietnam's 3,500-mile labyrinth of waterway
$6.95/$8.95 in Canada ISBN:0-553-34317

**Available at your local bookstore or call Bantam Books direct at
1-800-223-6834. (In New York State call 212-765-6500 ext.479.)**